CODE CHURN

MODERNIZATION INTELLIGENCE

Architecture as Strategic Infrastructure

A Practitioner's Handbook for Continuous Architectural Evolution

Code Churn

Software Modernization Intelligence

MODERNIZATION INTELLIGENCE

Architecture as Strategic Infrastructure

Published by Code Churn, LLC

codechurn.io

ISBN: 979-8-234-10775-6 (Paperback)

ISBN: 979-8-234-10775-6 (eBook)

First Edition, 2025

Printed in the United States of America

CONTENTS

Table of Contents

PART III — PUTTING IT INTO PRACTICE

Foreword

Every book about organizational change is, at some level, a book about the gap between what organizations know and what they do. The gap in this book is specific: most institutions that have invested seriously in software modernization know, from experience, that the approaches they have used have not produced the durable results they were intended to produce. They know this because they have lived through it — through the programs that delivered their defined scope and then watched the architecture slowly return to its prior condition, through the transformations that encountered complexity that was not in any plan, through the governance structures that could not maintain coherence through the organizational changes that occurred while the work was in progress.

This knowledge exists in most mature institutions. What is less available is the organizational framework to act on it — to translate the accumulated learning from years of modernization experience into a fundamentally different organizational approach. That is what this book is for.

Modernization Intelligence is not a new technology framework. It does not describe a new architectural pattern, a new platform, or a new engineering practice. It describes a new organizational model: a way of treating the continuous evolution of software architecture as a permanent institutional capability rather than as a periodic crisis response. The distinction matters because the failure mode of modernization — the pattern that repeats across industries, sectors, and organizational sizes — is not a failure of technology or engineering. It is a failure of organizational design.

Why this book exists

Code Churn was founded on a specific observation: that the most consequential challenges in software modernization are organizational, not technical. The technical problems of modernization are real and demanding, and the field has developed substantial capability for addressing them. What has not kept pace is the organizational capability to apply that technical knowledge effectively — to build the governance structures that sustain multi-year architectural investment, the institutional habits that make learning from modernization experience systematic, and the cultural conditions that allow honest assessment of what is and is not working.

This book is a synthesis of what we have learned working alongside institutions at every stage of the modernization journey: those beginning the foundational work of understanding their environments, those in the middle of complex transformation programs that have encountered the structural challenges this book describes, and those working to build the permanent modernization capability that makes continuous architectural evolution possible. The framework it presents — Modernization Intelligence — is not a theory. It is a distillation of organizational patterns that we have observed working, and organizational patterns that we have observed failing, across enough contexts to have reasonable confidence in the structural logic that distinguishes one from the other.

We have tried to write the book that we wished existed when we began this work — one that is specific enough to be actionable, honest enough to be credible, and grounded enough in organizational reality to be useful to the people who are actually doing the work rather than only to those who are planning it.

What this book is and is not

This book is a practitioner's handbook. It is written for the people who are responsible for building, leading, and sustaining modernization capability in real institutional contexts — people who need frameworks that are specific enough to apply, not general enough to be safe. It assumes a mixed readership: senior leaders who need the strategic and economic framing to govern modernization effectively, technical leaders who need the organizational design to build and run the modernization function, and practitioners who need the specific tools and practices to do the work.

This book is not a technical architecture guide. It does not describe specific platform choices, migration patterns, or engineering practices at the level of technical specification. Those resources exist in abundance, and the technical dimensions of modernization are far better served by domain-specific technical literature than by a handbook aimed at a mixed audience. What this book provides that technical literature does not is the organizational context in which technical decisions are made: the governance, the sequencing, the execution discipline, and the continuous evolution capability that determine whether sound technical decisions produce durable organizational outcomes.

This book is not a case study collection. While the archetypes and patterns described throughout draw on real organizational experience, specific institutions are not named and specific programs are not described. This is deliberate. The structural patterns that this book addresses are more useful as general frameworks than as specific narratives, and the organizational sensitivities around modernization are significant enough that anonymity serves both accuracy and candor.

This book is not a blueprint. Modernization Intelligence is a framework, not a formula. The specific organizational designs, governance structures, and investment models that the framework calls for vary by institutional context in ways that cannot be fully anticipated in a general handbook. What the book provides is the analytical structure for making good decisions about these specifics in your particular context, not a single set of answers that applies uniformly.

A note on the current moment

We are writing at a moment when the combination of rapidly advancing AI capabilities and decades of accumulated architectural debt is creating a particular kind of organizational pressure. The AI capabilities are real and in many cases genuinely useful for modernization work — Chapter Thirteen examines them honestly. The architectural debt is also real, and it is the primary constraint on organizations' ability to capitalize on AI and other emerging capabilities at the pace that competitive and operational pressures are demanding.

This convergence creates urgency that is genuine. Organizations that have not built the architectural adaptability required to integrate new capabilities continuously will find themselves at a compounding disadvantage relative to those that have. The investment required to build that adaptability — the Modernization Intelligence investment — is more consequential now than it has been at any previous point in the history of enterprise computing.

It also creates a specific risk that is worth naming at the outset. The availability of AI tools that can accelerate specific categories of modernization work has led some organizations to conclude that the organizational challenges of modernization are becoming less important — that if AI can do the technical work, the governance, the sequencing, and the continuous evolution capability are less necessary. This conclusion is false and potentially harmful. AI tools amplify the productivity of organizations that have built the organizational capability to apply them well. They do not substitute for that capability, and they do not make the governance, sequencing, and institutional habits described in this book less important. Chapter Thirteen makes this case in full.

How to read what follows

The book is organized in three parts and a conclusion. Part One makes the case for a different approach to modernization: why the current approaches have fallen short and what the structural reasons are. Part Two builds the Modernization Intelligence framework dimension by dimension, with the practical depth required to actually apply it. Part Three provides the diagnostic and implementation tools that translate the framework into organizational action.

Readers who are already convinced of the case and want to move directly to the framework can begin at Chapter Five. Readers who need the strategic and economic language to make the internal case for modernization investment will find the most useful material in Chapters One through Three. Readers who are building a modernization function from scratch should read Chapter Fourteen before the rest of Part Two, to understand the organizational context in which the framework operates.

The Reference Toolkit at the back of the book consolidates every diagnostic, assessment, and planning tool from all fourteen chapters into a single working reference. It is designed to be used — in workshops, in governance conversations, in team assessments — not just read.

We hope the book is useful. More than that, we hope the organizations that read it build something with it.

Code Churn

Software Modernization Intelligence

NAVIGATION GUIDE

How to Use This Book

This handbook is designed to be used, not just read. It contains fourteen chapters, a conclusion, a comprehensive reference toolkit, and a glossary — enough material that reading it straight through from beginning to end is one approach, but not necessarily the most useful one for every reader. This section describes the book's structure, maps different reader types to the content most directly relevant to them, and explains how the diagnostic and planning tools are intended to be applied.

The structure at a glance

The book is organized in three parts, each with a distinct purpose.

Part One (Chapters 1–4) makes the case for a different approach to modernization. It describes the structural reality of modern software environments, examines the economic and strategic costs of architectural constraint, and analyzes the structural failure patterns that have caused traditional modernization programs to fall short. This part is primarily diagnostic: it is designed to build the shared organizational understanding that effective modernization requires, including the language and the evidence base needed to make the internal case for sustained architectural investment.

Part Two (Chapters 5–10) builds the Modernization Intelligence framework. Each chapter takes one of the five dimensions — architectural awareness, transformation sequencing, execution discipline, governance alignment, and continuous evolution — and works through the specific practices, tools, and organizational designs required to build that dimension as a genuine organizational capability. This part is the operational core of the handbook.

Part Three (Chapters 11–14) provides the implementation tools. The maturity assessment in Chapter Eleven scores your organization across all five framework dimensions. The archetype analysis in Chapter Twelve helps identify the primary structural character of your modernization challenge. Chapter Thirteen examines AI tools with the clear-eyed assessment they deserve. Chapter Fourteen is a practical guide to building the modernization function itself.

The Reference Toolkit consolidates every diagnostic, checklist, and planning template from all fourteen chapters. The Glossary defines the twenty-two terms used with specific meanings throughout the book.

Reading paths by role

Senior executives and board members

If you are a CEO, COO, board member, or equivalent, your most direct value is in understanding why architecture has become a strategic leadership concern, what the economic stakes are, and what the governance commitment looks like from the leadership position.

Recommended path: Read Chapters 1, 3, and 4 in full. These establish the strategic framing, the economic case, and the organizational failure patterns that a different approach addresses. Then read Chapter 9 (governance alignment) and Chapter 14 (building the modernization function) to understand what the organizational commitment looks like at your level. The Conclusion provides the institutional argument in its most direct form.

Tools most relevant to your role: Tool 1.1 (strategic conversation diagnostic), Tool 1.3 (friction cost framework), Tool 2.5 (governance design worksheet), Tool 2.6 (governance health check), Tool 3.4 (function charter template).

Chief technology officers and VPs of Engineering

If you are the senior technology leader responsible for the modernization function or for building it, this book is written primarily for you. You need both the strategic framing to lead the governance conversations and the operational depth to build and run the capability.

Recommended path: Read Parts One and Two in full. Then use Chapter 11 to assess where your organization currently stands, Chapter 12 to identify your primary archetype, and Chapter 14 for the organizational design guidance. The expanded Chapter 9 and Chapter 10 (in the manuscript, they appear twice — once in the standard Part II flow and once as expanded standalone chapters) are particularly important reading for the governance and continuous evolution dimensions.

Tools most relevant to your role: Full MI Maturity Assessment (Tool 3.1), Governance Design Worksheet (Tool 2.5), Continuous Evolution Readiness Assessment (Tool 2.7), Function Charter Template (Tool 3.4), First-Year Roadmap (Tool 3.5).

Architects and senior practitioners

If you are a principal architect, lead architect, or senior practitioner doing the technical work of modernization, the most directly applicable content is in Part Two. Chapters 6, 7, and 8 (awareness, sequencing, execution) are the practitioner chapters. Chapter 11's scoring tables are designed to be used by a technical team assessing their own capability.

Recommended path: Read Chapter 5 for the framework overview, then work through Chapters 6, 7, and 8 in sequence. Use Chapter 11 to score your current capability across each dimension and identify the highest-priority investments. Chapter 12's archetype framework will help you connect the structural character of your challenge to the approaches that have worked in similar situations.

Tools most relevant to your role: Architectural Awareness Assessment (Tool 2.2), Sequencing Decision Checklist (Tool 2.3),

Execution Readiness Checklist (Tool 2.4), the full scoring tables in Chapter 11.

Consultants and modernization advisors

If you are advising institutions on modernization strategy, the full book is relevant reading. The framework provides the analytical structure for diagnostic engagements, the archetype framework provides a rapid situational classifier, and the governance and continuous evolution chapters provide the organizational design language that most client conversations require.

Recommended path: Read the full book in sequence. The maturity assessment in Chapter 11 is designed to be administered as a facilitated workshop with client leadership teams — it works most effectively when the scoring is done collaboratively rather than individually. The archetype framework in Chapter 12 can be used as a rapid diagnostic at the beginning of an engagement to focus attention on the primary structural challenge.

Tools most relevant to your role: All Part I tools for diagnostic framing, the full MI Maturity Assessment for capability assessment, the Archetype Identification Diagnostic, the Governance Design Worksheet, and the Function Charter Template.

Using the diagnostic tools

The diagnostic tools throughout the book are designed to be used in organizational contexts, not just as reading material. Each tool is reproduced in full in the Reference Toolkit at the back of the book, in a format designed for use in meetings, workshops, and planning sessions.

Three principles guide effective use of the tools. First, use them collaboratively. The most valuable diagnostic outputs come from scoring discussions in which different members of the leadership team arrive at different scores and must discuss the evidence behind their assessments. The disagreements are often more informative than the consensus scores.

Second, treat scores as directional, not precise. The maturity assessment and the other scoring tools are instruments for generating useful organizational conversations, not for producing authoritative capability measurements. A score of 11 versus 12 on any dimension is not meaningful. The difference between a score of 7 and a score of 16 is very meaningful. Use the tools to identify patterns and gaps, not to produce numbers.

Third, connect tool outputs to decisions. The tools are only valuable if their outputs inform organizational decisions: about where to invest, what to prioritize, and what governance commitments to make. Every tool use should conclude with a specific decision or a specific next step. If the output of a diagnostic session is a set of scores that get filed and not acted on, the tool has not served its purpose.

A word on sequencing

Readers who work through the book will encounter repeated emphasis on the importance of sequencing in modernization work. The same principle applies to using the book itself. The most effective use of this handbook is not to attempt all of the framework dimensions simultaneously, but to understand where you are, identify the highest-leverage investments, and build sequentially from there.

The starting position diagnostic in Chapter Five is the right entry point for organizations beginning to build Modernization Intelligence. The maturity assessment in Chapter Eleven is the right entry point for organizations that want a comprehensive picture of their current capability profile. Either starting point will produce a map of where to focus first, and that map is the most important output the book can provide.

The framework is a system, and systems are built over time. Organizations that attempt to implement all five dimensions at once will find themselves overwhelmed. Organizations that identify the two or three highest-leverage investments and execute them with discipline, before moving to the next level, will find that each round of investment makes the next round more effective. That compounding dynamic is not just a principle of the Modernization Intelligence framework. It is the operating logic of this handbook as well.

Modernization is no longer an improvement initiative.

It is a defining condition of institutional effectiveness.

PART ONE

The Case for Change

Understanding why software architecture has become the defining condition of institutional effectiveness — and why the traditional response to that condition has fallen short.

CHAPTER 1

Architecture as Strategic Infrastructure

Why the condition of your software environment is no longer an IT concern — and what it means for how institutions are led

---

There is a conversation that happens in boardrooms, executive committees, and leadership offsites with increasing frequency. It begins with something concrete — a delayed product launch, a compliance gap, an integration project that has consumed eighteen months and still isn't done — and it ends in the same place every time. Someone at the table asks why these things keep happening, and someone else explains, carefully, that the underlying technology environment is more constrained than people realize. The systems are old, or the integrations are complex, or the technical debt has accumulated to a point where straightforward changes require extraordinary effort.

The conversation is usually received with a mixture of concern and frustration. Concern because the constraint is real and its consequences are beginning to compound. Frustration because this doesn't feel like a new problem — it feels like a problem that was supposed to have been solved already, by the last transformation program, or the one before that.

This handbook begins with that conversation because it is the right starting point. Not because the frustration is misplaced — it isn't — but because the way the problem tends to get framed in that room is itself part of why it persists. The conversation is almost always about technology: about which systems are outdated, which platforms need to be replaced, which integrations need to be rebuilt. What it rarely is, at least not explicitly, is a conversation about organizational capability — about whether the institution has developed the sustained ability to manage its own technological environment as a strategic asset.

That reframing is what this book is about. Software architecture, in modern institutions, has become strategic infrastructure. It is not peripheral to institutional performance. It is constitutive of it. And the work of managing that infrastructure — the discipline of continuous architectural evolution — is not a technical function. It is an organizational capability that must be built, governed, and developed with the same intentionality that institutions bring to their most important strategic assets.

What strategic infrastructure actually means

The term strategic infrastructure is used in specific ways in institutional management. Physical infrastructure — roads, electrical grids, telecommunications networks — is understood to be the enabling condition for economic activity. You can't run a logistics operation without roads. You can't operate a data center without reliable power. The infrastructure doesn't do the work; it makes the work possible. And the quality of the infrastructure determines the range and cost of the work that can be done.

Software architecture functions the same way, at the institutional level. It is the enabling condition for institutional activity. An organization's ability to serve its customers, comply with its regulatory obligations, integrate with its partners, and respond to changes in its environment is determined, to a degree that is rarely fully appreciated, by the condition of its software systems. Those systems are not just tools. They are infrastructure — the substrate on which institutional operations run.

The strategic implication follows directly. Institutions that maintain high-quality infrastructure retain more operational freedom than those that do not. They can pursue a wider range of activities, respond to a wider range of demands, and adapt to a wider range of conditions. Institutions that neglect infrastructure find their operational freedom contracting, often slowly and then suddenly, as accumulated degradation crosses thresholds that begin to constrain operations in ways that cannot be compensated for at the surface.

For most of the history of enterprise computing, it was possible for senior leaders to treat software architecture as a background concern — something important enough to fund but not important enough to personally understand or govern. The pace of change was slow enough, and the tolerance for workarounds high enough, that the consequences of architectural neglect were manageable. That is no longer true in most institutional contexts. The pace of external change — in regulation, in competitive dynamics, in customer and citizen expectations, in technology itself — has accelerated to the point where architectural constraint translates directly into strategic constraint, often within timescales that are shorter than typical planning cycles.

> *The organizations that understand this — that treat software architecture as the strategic infrastructure it has become — are developing a fundamental advantage over those that do not. Not because they have better technology, but because they have built the organizational capability to manage and evolve their technology environment continuously.*

The leadership gap

One of the more persistent challenges in this domain is that the people who are most affected by architectural constraint are often the people least well-positioned to diagnose it or address it directly. Senior leaders experience the consequences — delayed initiatives, frustrated customers, compliance exposure, budget overruns — without having reliable frameworks for connecting those consequences to their architectural causes. Technical leaders understand the causes but often lack the organizational authority, the executive relationships, or the strategic framing required to address them at the appropriate level.

The result is a persistent gap between where the problem lives and where it gets managed. Architectural constraint is a strategic problem that gets managed as a technical problem. It is addressed through IT budgets, project portfolios, and vendor relationships rather than through the leadership conversations, organizational investments, and governance structures that strategic problems require.

This handbook is written for both sides of that gap. For senior leaders, it provides the conceptual framework and the organizational language to engage with architectural questions as the strategic questions they are — not to make them into technical experts, but to make them into informed governors of a capability that significantly determines institutional performance. For technical leaders, architects, and practitioners, it provides a structured approach to building the organizational capability — the Modernization Intelligence — that makes continuous architectural evolution possible.

The two audiences need each other. The organizational capability cannot be built without senior leadership engagement and commitment. The senior leadership engagement will not be meaningful without technical leaders who can translate architectural complexity into strategic terms. Building the bridge between these two perspectives is one of the central practical challenges that this handbook addresses.

Introducing Modernization Intelligence

Modernization Intelligence is the institutional capability that determines whether an organization can evolve its software environment without losing strategic momentum. It is defined as a capability rather than a methodology deliberately. A methodology is a set of steps. A capability is something an organization becomes able to do — continuously, reliably, and with improving effectiveness over time.

The distinction matters because the failure mode of modernization is almost never a failure of steps. Organizations know roughly what modernization involves: assess the current environment, define a target state, build a migration plan, execute the migration, validate the results. The steps are not mysterious. What fails is the organizational capacity to execute those steps reliably, to maintain strategic coherence across multi-year timelines, to learn from execution and apply those lessons forward, and to sustain the work as a continuous discipline rather than treating each round of modernization as a self-contained project.

Modernization Intelligence is composed of five integrated dimensions: architectural awareness, transformation sequencing, execution discipline, governance alignment, and continuous evolution. These are not stages or phases. They are simultaneous, mutually reinforcing aspects of a single organizational capability that must be developed together. An organization with excellent architectural awareness but weak governance will make good diagnoses and poor decisions. An organization with strong execution discipline but inadequate sequencing will implement changes efficiently in the wrong order. Each dimension depends on the others, and the full capability is realized only when all five are functioning as an integrated system.

This handbook works through each dimension in detail, with the practical specificity that practitioners need to actually build it. But before we get to the how, we need to fully understand the why — the structural realities of modern software environments, the economic and strategic consequences of architectural constraint, and the patterns that have made traditional modernization approaches insufficient. That is the work of Part One.

How to read this book

This handbook is written for a mixed audience, and different readers will come to it with different needs and different starting points. Before moving to Chapter Two, it is worth being explicit about how the book is structured and how different readers might navigate it.

Senior executives and board members will find the most direct value in Chapters One through Four — the strategic and economic framing of the problem — and in Chapters Nine and Eleven, which address governance and organizational maturity assessment respectively. Chapter Fourteen, which covers building the modernization function, is important reading for any leader who will be asked to sponsor or fund this capability.

Chief technology officers, VPs of Engineering, and senior architects will find the greatest depth in Chapters Five through Ten, which build the full Modernization Intelligence framework dimension by dimension. These chapters are where the conceptual framework of the earlier sections is translated into organizational practice.

Practitioners — architects, engineers, delivery leads, and program managers — will find the most directly applicable material in the practitioner tools embedded throughout Chapters Six through Ten, and in the Reference Toolkit at the back of the book. These tools are designed to be used in the actual work of modernization, not merely read.

Consultants and advisors will likely want to read the full book in sequence. The framework is coherent across its parts, and the diagnostic tools in Part Three are more useful when grounded in the analytical depth of Parts One and Two.

Throughout the book, boxes labeled 'Practitioner Note' contain specific guidance for people implementing the concepts in real organizational contexts. Boxes labeled 'Leadership Note' contain framing and language specifically designed for executive and governance conversations. Diagnostic tools and worksheets are clearly marked and designed to be applied directly.

The book is not prescriptive about organizational size or industry. The principles and frameworks apply across contexts — large institutions and mid-sized ones, public sector and private, technology-intensive and traditionally less so. Where guidance needs to be calibrated to context, the book provides the calibration framework rather than a single answer.

The work of modernization is never finished — which means the organization that treats it as finished has, in effect, decided to let its architectural condition degrade until the next crisis forces it back to the table.

DIAGNOSTIC — IS ARCHITECTURE A STRATEGIC CONVERSATION IN YOUR ORGANIZATION?

Before moving to Chapter Two, consider where software architecture currently sits in your institution's governance and strategic conversations. The following questions are not scored — they are intended to locate you in relation to the challenge this book addresses.

Does your executive committee have a shared language for discussing architectural condition and its strategic implications, or does the conversation typically stay at the level of project status and IT budget?

When a major strategic initiative is planned — a new product, a market expansion, a regulatory compliance program — does the discussion explicitly address whether the current architecture can support it, and at what cost and timeline?

Is there a senior leader in your organization who has both the technical credibility to understand architectural condition and the organizational authority to address it at the strategic level? If so, are they in the right governance conversations?

When modernization programs have been undertaken in your organization, have they produced durable improvement in architectural condition, or has the environment gradually returned to its prior state within a few years of program completion?

If you found yourself unable to answer several of these questions, or found the answers uncomfortable, that is useful information. Most organizations are at an early stage of treating architecture as a strategic concern. This book is designed to help you move forward from wherever you are.

CHAPTER 2

The Real Shape of Modern Software Environments

What your technology environment actually looks like — and why the gap between that reality and how it's discussed creates persistent difficulty

---

Before an institution can develop a sound modernization strategy, it needs an accurate picture of what it is working with. This sounds obvious, and in most organizations it is treated as obvious — the assumption being that leadership already understands the environment well enough to make strategic decisions about it. In practice, the gap between the assumed picture and the actual picture is one of the most consequential sources of modernization difficulty.

The assumed picture tends to look like this: there are some legacy systems that need to be replaced, there are some modern systems that are working well, and there is a roadmap for gradually migrating from the former to the latter. Progress is being made, even if slowly. The environment is messy but understood.

The actual picture is usually more complex. Legacy systems are more deeply embedded than the assumed picture suggests, and the dependencies that connect them to the rest of the environment are denser and less documented than anyone fully appreciates. The modern systems are less modern than they appear — many are only a few years from becoming the next generation of legacy. The integrations that connect everything together are numerous, fragile, and poorly understood. And the gap between documented architecture and actual operational behavior is wide enough to surprise even the most experienced technical teams when they begin significant change work.

This chapter establishes an accurate picture of modern institutional software environments. Not as a counsel of despair — the environments that most institutions are working with are manageable — but as a necessary foundation for the chapters that follow. Sound modernization strategy requires honest engagement with the real shape of the problem.

The permanent hybrid environment

The most important single thing to understand about modern institutional software environments is that they are hybrid — containing multiple generations of technology operating simultaneously — and that this hybrid condition is permanent rather than transitional.

This is a harder claim to accept than it might appear. Most technology planning frameworks assume that the hybrid state is temporary: that the organization is in the process of migrating from older platforms to newer ones, and that the transition will eventually complete. This assumption shapes investment decisions, governance structures, and organizational expectations in ways that consistently make modernization harder than it needs to be.

The hybrid condition is permanent for structural reasons. Software systems are built to serve operational needs, and they serve those needs until the cost of maintaining them or the risk of running them exceeds the cost and risk of replacing them. For many core institutional systems, that threshold is never reached — or is reached only after decades. The mainframe that processes pension payments reliably and cost-effectively does not get replaced because it is old. It gets replaced only when the operational case for replacement becomes compelling relative to the risk and cost of executing it. For many systems, that case never becomes compelling enough during the system's operational life.

Simultaneously, technology evolves. New platforms, new patterns, and new capabilities emerge continuously. Institutions adopt them selectively — for new capabilities, for specific domains where the case is clear, for requirements that existing systems cannot meet. The result, over any significant period, is an environment in which multiple generations of technology coexist: the mainframes of the 1980s alongside the client-server systems of the 1990s alongside the web applications of the 2000s alongside the cloud services of the 2010s alongside the AI-enabled capabilities being introduced today.

Each of these generations is present in most mature institutional environments, and each will remain present for the foreseeable future. The practical implication for modernization strategy is significant: planning for a future state in which the environment is architecturally uniform is planning for a state that will not exist. The productive planning target is not uniformity but manageability — a hybrid environment that is well understood, appropriately integrated, and capable of selective evolution without systemic disruption.

Understanding legacy systems honestly

The word 'legacy' has acquired a heavily negative connotation in technology discussions — it is associated with obsolescence, risk, cost, and constraint. This connotation is not entirely unwarranted. Legacy systems do impose real limitations, and those limitations do create real costs. But the exclusively negative framing causes organizations to systematically undervalue something that legacy systems contain in abundance: accumulated institutional knowledge.

A core transaction processing system that has operated for thirty years has been modified, extended, and refined in response to thousands of real-world conditions. Edge cases that were discovered in year three have been handled in code that has been running ever since. Regulatory changes from fifteen years ago have been incorporated into logic that nobody fully remembers writing but that runs correctly every day. Business rules that were the subject of intense organizational debate two decades ago are now encoded in system behavior that simply works — and whose logic would be difficult to reconstruct from any other source.

This accumulated knowledge is not just historically interesting. It is operationally critical. It represents the institution's understanding of its own domain, encoded in software over decades of real-world operation. When organizations replace legacy systems without first understanding and capturing this embedded knowledge, they do not modernize — they amputate institutional memory and spend the following years discovering what they have lost, usually in the form of production failures, customer complaints, and regulatory findings that the new system handles incorrectly.

A more honest and ultimately more productive framing of legacy systems treats them as repositories of institutional knowledge that happen to be running on aging technology. The goal is not to eliminate them as quickly as possible but to understand them thoroughly enough to evolve them safely — to extract the knowledge they contain, transfer the capabilities they provide to more current platforms where that transfer is warranted, and retire them only when the operational case for doing so is clear and the knowledge transfer is complete.

This framing also changes the work of modernization. The most important early work is not technical — it is analytical. It is the work of understanding what legacy systems actually do, what they know, and what depends on them. Organizations that invest in this work consistently make better modernization decisions and encounter fewer surprises. Organizations that skip it in favor of moving quickly to implementation consistently encounter the cost of that shortcut in ways that more than offset whatever time was saved.

The dependency landscape

If legacy systems are the most misunderstood component of institutional software environments, the dependency landscape is the most underestimated source of modernization complexity. Dependencies — the integration relationships, data flows, behavioral couplings, and operational interdependencies that connect systems to one another — accumulate continuously in institutional environments and are rarely fully understood by anyone.

Understanding the full scope of the dependency problem requires distinguishing between three types of dependencies that operate differently and are discovered differently.

Explicit technical dependencies are the integrations that are formally designed and at least partially documented: APIs, data feeds, message queues, batch file transfers, shared databases. These are the dependencies that appear on architecture diagrams and that technical teams are aware of. They are not always well documented — the documentation is frequently incomplete or out of date — but they are at least visible enough to be examined.

Implicit behavioral dependencies are more dangerous. They arise when one system has come to rely on specific behaviors of another system that are not formally specified or documented. A downstream system may depend on a particular response time from an upstream system, not because that response time is specified anywhere but because the downstream system's timeout logic was written with that assumption. A batch process may depend on another process completing by a specific time, not because the dependency is documented but because the sequencing was established years ago and nobody has questioned it since. These dependencies are invisible until they break — until a change to one system causes an unexpected failure in another.

Organizational dependencies are different in kind from both of the above. They are not technical at all; they are the business processes, operational workflows, and human procedures that have been designed around specific system behaviors. A claims adjudication team may have developed a workflow that depends on a specific field being formatted in a specific way in the legacy system. A reporting team may have built analytical processes that depend on data being available at a specific time each morning. When the underlying systems change, these organizational dependencies create constraints that are not visible in any technical analysis of the environment.

PRACTITIONER NOTE — THE DEPENDENCY AUDIT

Most organizations significantly underestimate the density of their dependency landscape until they attempt a significant modernization effort and encounter what they missed. A dependency audit conducted before major transformation work is one of the highest-leverage investments a modernization function can make.

An effective dependency audit has three components. The first is automated technical discovery: using static analysis tools, network monitoring, and integration platform logs to map the explicit technical integrations that exist in the environment. This is a starting point, not a complete picture.

The second is operational interviews: structured conversations with the people who operate, support, and depend on the systems being audited. These conversations surface implicit behavioral dependencies and organizational dependencies that automated tools cannot detect. The questions to ask are not 'what does this system integrate with?' but 'what breaks when this system behaves differently than expected?' and 'what do people do when this system is unavailable?'

The third is historical failure analysis: examining the change history of the systems in scope and identifying patterns in what broke when changes were made. Past failures are the most reliable indicator of implicit dependencies that formal analysis has missed.

The output of a dependency audit is not a complete map — no map of a mature institutional environment will ever be complete — but a sufficiently accurate picture of the dependency landscape to make confident sequencing decisions. Chapter

Seven covers how to use this output in transformation sequencing.

Why complexity grows geometrically

One of the most important things to understand about dependency accumulation is that it does not grow linearly with the size of the environment. It grows geometrically. Each new system added to an environment creates potential coupling points with every other system it must interact with. Each integration creates new dependencies. Each middleware layer — introduced to manage the proliferation of point-to-point integrations — adds its own complexity and its own coupling.

In a simple environment with five systems, the maximum number of pairwise dependency relationships is ten. In an environment with twenty systems, the maximum is one hundred ninety. In an environment with fifty systems, the maximum is twelve hundred twenty-five. Real environments are not fully connected — not every system depends on every other — but the scaling relationship holds. As environments grow, their dependency complexity grows far faster than the number of systems would suggest.

The practical consequence is that dependency complexity in mature institutional environments is genuinely beyond the capacity of any individual or team to fully comprehend. This is not a failure of intelligence or attention — it is a structural feature of the environment. Managing complexity that exceeds individual comprehension requires organizational mechanisms: systematic documentation practices, dependency analysis tooling, architectural governance structures, and the organizational habits that ensure dependency knowledge is maintained as the environment evolves.

Organizations that lack these mechanisms rely on the tacit knowledge of experienced individuals — the architects and engineers who have worked in the environment for years and have accumulated, through experience, an intuitive understanding of its dependencies. This knowledge is valuable, but it is fragile. It walks out the door when experienced people leave. It cannot be shared across teams. And it degrades as the environment changes in ways that outpace anyone's ability to keep their mental model current.

Building organizational mechanisms for dependency understanding — the tools, practices, and governance structures that make architectural knowledge a shared institutional asset rather than an individual one — is one of the foundational investments that Modernization Intelligence requires. Chapter Six covers this in detail.

The integration layer as a first-class architectural domain

In most institutional software environments, the integration layer — the collection of APIs, middleware platforms, message brokers, data pipelines, and event streams that connect systems to one another — is treated as a supporting concern rather than a primary one. Systems are designed first; integrations are built to connect them. This ordering of priority has produced integration landscapes that are, in many institutions, more complex and more fragile than the application systems they connect.

The integration layer in a mature institutional environment is typically a geological record of the institution's technology history. There are point-to-point integrations built in the 1990s, file-transfer-based integrations built in the 2000s, enterprise service bus integrations built in the 2010s, REST APIs built more recently, and real-time event streams introduced in the last few years. Each generation was introduced to solve a problem with the previous generation. Each has accumulated its own dependencies. And the whole has become a system of systems whose complexity exceeds what any single team understands.

Managing this landscape effectively requires treating integration architecture as a first-class architectural domain — not as an afterthought to application design but as a primary concern that deserves dedicated expertise, explicit governance, and continuous investment. The organizations that do this find that their integration layer becomes a source of architectural coherence: a well-designed integration platform simplifies the work of adding new systems, retiring old ones, and changing the behavior of the environment overall. The organizations that don't find that their integration layer becomes the primary obstacle to every modernization effort they undertake.

The documented architecture versus the actual architecture

There is almost always a gap between the documented architecture and the actual architecture in mature institutional environments. The documented architecture is the one that appears in diagrams, wikis, and architectural decision records. The actual architecture is the one that processes transactions, serves customers, and runs in production. The gap between them is one of the most reliable sources of surprise in modernization work.

The gap exists for several reasons. Documentation is created at points in time and then not updated as the environment changes. The people responsible for maintaining documentation have operational priorities that consistently take precedence over documentation work. Systems are modified in ways that are not reflected in architectural records — a quick integration built to solve an immediate problem, a database change that creates an undocumented coupling, a configuration modification that alters system behavior in ways that no diagram captures.

The practical implication for modernization is that architectural discovery — the work of understanding the actual state of the environment — cannot be shortcut by reviewing existing documentation. Documentation is a starting point, not a substitute for direct analysis. The organizations that discover this late in a transformation effort, after having made significant investments based on an inaccurate understanding of the environment, pay a steep price for the shortcut.

DIAGNOSTIC — ENVIRONMENTAL CLARITY ASSESSMENT

The following questions are designed to help you assess the clarity of your organization's understanding of its current software environment. Score each question on a scale of 1 to 4, where 1 means 'we have no reliable answer to this' and 4 means 'we have a current, accurate, and widely shared answer to this'.

Can you identify, with confidence, all of the production systems in your environment — including shadow IT and locally maintained tools that carry real operational load?

Do you have a current and accurate map of the integration relationships between your core systems — including implicit behavioral dependencies, not just formally documented APIs?

Do you know which systems, if they were unavailable for 24 hours, would cause the most significant operational impact — and have you tested those dependencies recently?

When a change is proposed to a core system, do you have reliable mechanisms for assessing the likely downstream effects before the change is implemented?

Is your architectural documentation current enough to be useful for modernization planning, or is it primarily a historical record of how systems were designed rather than how they currently operate?

Score interpretation: 16–20: Strong environmental clarity — a solid foundation for modernization planning. 10–15: Partial clarity — significant gaps that should be addressed before major transformation commitments. Below 10: Low clarity — the dependency audit described above should be a near-term priority before significant modernization investment is made.

CHAPTER 3

What Architectural Friction Actually Costs

Moving beyond the IT budget conversation to understand the full economic and strategic cost of operating in a constrained environment

---

There is a number that most institutions know: the cost of their IT operations. It appears in annual budgets, board reports, and technology strategy presentations. It includes staff costs, infrastructure costs, software licensing costs, and the cost of the programs and projects that make up the technology portfolio. It is, in most organizations, a large number — and it has been growing.

What most institutions do not know, or do not know with any precision, is the cost of architectural friction — the additional cost imposed on the institution by operating a software environment that cannot efficiently support the demands placed on it. This cost is real, it is substantial, and it is almost entirely invisible in standard financial reporting. Making it visible is one of the most important things a modernization leader can do to build the organizational commitment that sustained architectural investment requires.

This chapter provides the frameworks for doing that. It describes the major categories of architectural friction cost, explains how they accumulate and compound, and offers a practical approach for estimating their magnitude in your own organization. It also addresses the strategic dimension of architectural constraint — the effects on strategic optionality and organizational adaptability that are harder to quantify but no less real.

The direct costs: what you can measure

The most tractable architectural friction costs are those that can be connected to specific budget lines or operational metrics. They include maintenance burden, rework costs, and the cost of manual compensations.

Maintenance burden is the proportion of technology investment that is consumed by keeping existing systems running rather than building new capability. In organizations with healthy architectural environments, this proportion is typically in the range of thirty to forty percent. In organizations with significant architectural debt — complex, aging environments with dense dependencies and limited documentation — maintenance can consume sixty to eighty percent of the technology budget, leaving very little for the new development and capability building that operational and strategic demands require.

The maintenance burden is not fixed. It grows as environments age and as changes make them more complex. A system that required twenty percent of a team's capacity to maintain five years ago may require forty percent today, not because it has been significantly extended but because its dependencies have grown, its documentation has degraded, and the team's understanding of its behavior has narrowed as experienced staff have left. This growth is gradual and largely invisible until it reaches a threshold where it begins to constrain the team's ability to deliver anything else.

Rework costs arise from changes that are made incorrectly — because the dependency landscape was not fully understood, because testing was inadequate to catch the full scope of change consequences, or because the architecture made it difficult to isolate the change from unintended effects. In environments with high dependency complexity, rework is endemic. Projects that should take three months take nine. Releases that are planned for a Friday are delayed to the following month because a dependency that was not on anyone's radar broke in testing. The cumulative cost of this rework, across an organization's full portfolio of modernization and development work, is enormous — but it is almost never tracked as a category in financial reporting.

Manual compensations are the operational workarounds that have been introduced to compensate for things the software environment cannot do automatically. A compliance team that manually reconciles two systems because an integration does not exist. A customer service team that re-enters data from one system into another because they are not connected. A finance team that runs a monthly extract-and-reload process because the reporting system cannot access data from the operational system directly. These compensations are operational costs — staff time, error risk, process complexity — that are invisible as architectural costs. They appear in departmental budgets as headcount or contractor spend, not as technology infrastructure costs. But they are, in origin, architectural friction costs.

The indirect costs: what you can estimate

Beyond the direct costs that can be connected to specific operational activities, architectural friction generates indirect costs that are more difficult to measure precisely but often larger in aggregate magnitude. These include delayed delivery, foregone opportunity, and regulatory exposure.

Delayed delivery is the cost of capabilities and services that reach customers, citizens, or internal users later than they should because architectural constraint slowed the development process. In competitive markets, delayed delivery translates directly into foregone revenue and market share. In regulated industries, it can mean failing to meet service commitments or compliance timelines. In public sector contexts, it means citizens or beneficiaries receiving services later than they should.

The challenge with delayed delivery as a cost category is that the counterfactual — what would have been delivered if the architecture had been better — is inherently speculative. But it is possible to estimate the cost of specific delays where the business impact is identifiable. A product launch delayed by six months due to integration complexity can be costed based on the revenue trajectory of comparable products. A compliance deadline missed because legacy systems could not support the required reporting can be costed based on the regulatory consequences. These are not precise numbers, but they are credible enough to anchor an organizational conversation about the cost of architectural constraint.

Foregone opportunity costs are more diffuse but potentially more significant. They arise when the architecture prevents the organization from pursuing strategic directions that would otherwise be attractive — when a partnership cannot be formed because the integration complexity is too high, when a new market cannot be entered because the systems required to serve it cannot be built on the existing platform, when an acquisition cannot be integrated because the combining of two already complex environments would create an unmanageable whole.

Every strategic option that an organization cannot pursue because its architecture will not support it represents a real cost — even though that cost never appears in any budget.

These foregone opportunities are invisible in standard financial reporting because they represent things that did not happen. But they are real costs — real reductions in institutional value — and they compound over time as the cumulative effect of many individual foregone options narrows the strategic range available to the organization.

The strategic cost: optionality and adaptability

Beyond the costs that can be estimated in financial terms, architectural constraint imposes costs on institutional capability that are fundamentally strategic rather than financial. The most important of these is the erosion of strategic optionality.

Strategic optionality is the range of viable directions available to an institution — the set of things it could do if circumstances warranted. It is the organizational equivalent of liquidity: the capacity to move, to respond, to change course when conditions require. Institutions with high strategic optionality can adapt to unexpected challenges and capitalize on unexpected opportunities. Institutions with low strategic optionality are locked into their current trajectory regardless of what changes around them.

Software architecture is a significant determinant of strategic optionality. An institution whose systems can be reconfigured, extended, and integrated with new capabilities has a wide range of viable strategic directions. An institution whose systems are brittle, tightly coupled, and resistant to change has a narrow range — and that range contracts further every year that architectural debt is allowed to accumulate.

The erosion of optionality is particularly consequential in environments of rapid external change. Regulatory requirements can shift faster than organizations with constrained architectures can respond. Competitive disruption can emerge from directions that require the integration of capabilities that the current architecture cannot support. Customer and citizen expectations can shift in ways that demand new service delivery models that legacy systems were not designed to provide. In all of these cases, the institutions that can respond are those whose architectures support rapid reconfiguration. The institutions that cannot respond are not failing because of strategy, talent, or intent. They are failing because the infrastructure required to execute a response does not have the flexibility to support it.

A framework for estimating architectural friction cost

Given the mix of measurable, estimable, and inherently qualitative costs involved, how should an organization approach quantifying the cost of architectural friction for internal decision-making purposes? The following framework provides a practical approach that can be executed without specialized financial modeling tools.

Step 1 — Quantify the maintenance burden gap

Begin with the IT operations budget and identify the proportion consumed by maintaining existing systems versus delivering new capability. Compare this to a target ratio appropriate to your industry and scale — for most organizations, a healthy ratio has roughly sixty percent of technology investment directed toward new capability and forty percent toward maintenance. If your ratio is inverted, the excess maintenance spend above the target ratio is a conservative estimate of direct architectural friction cost.

Step 2 — Catalog and cost delayed deliveries

Review the past two to three years of technology project delivery and identify the projects that were significantly delayed relative to original estimates. For each, estimate the business cost of the delay — in revenue, compliance exposure, or service quality terms. Sum these costs across the portfolio. This gives you a floor estimate for the direct business cost of architectural constraint on delivery velocity.

Step 3 — Inventory manual compensations

Survey the operational departments that work with or depend on the systems in scope. Ask them to identify the manual processes they run to compensate for integration gaps, data quality issues, or system limitations. For each process identified, estimate the annual staff cost. This is a category that consistently surprises people — the aggregate cost of manual compensations in large institutional environments routinely reaches into the tens of millions of dollars annually.

Step 4 — Identify foregone strategic opportunities

Review the past few years of strategic discussions — board presentations, executive committee discussions, business development conversations — and identify cases where a strategic option was declined or constrained because of architectural concerns. For each, make a rough estimate of the value of the foregone option. This is the most subjective part of the analysis, but it is also often the largest category when properly examined.

> **LEADERSHIP NOTE — MAKING THE CASE FOR MODERNIZATION INVESTMENT**
>
> The framework above is designed to produce a defensible internal estimate of the cost of architectural constraint — one that can anchor a leadership conversation about why sustained modernization investment is justified.
>
> A few guidance points for using it effectively. First, be honest about uncertainty. The estimates in categories two through four are inherently approximate, and presenting them as precise numbers will undermine rather than build credibility. Present them as ranges with explicit assumptions, and let the aggregate picture make the argument rather than any single number.
>
> Second, focus on trends. The absolute cost at a point in time is less compelling than the trajectory. If maintenance costs as a proportion of technology budget have increased from forty percent to sixty percent over the past five years, that trend, projected forward, is the strongest possible argument for sustained architectural investment.
>
> Third, connect to specific strategic stakes. Abstract arguments about technical debt are less persuasive than concrete arguments about specific strategic priorities that are at risk. If the organization's top strategic priority for the next three years requires capabilities that the current architecture cannot support without significant investment, that specific connection is the most powerful argument available.

The compounding dynamic

Perhaps the most important economic characteristic of architectural friction is that it compounds. An environment with moderate architectural debt will accumulate more debt over time, even without any neglect, simply because the complexity of the environment makes every change more expensive and more prone to creating unintended side effects. As changes are made to address business needs, they add to the integration complexity. As new capabilities are built on a fragile foundation, they inherit the fragility and extend it. As the environment grows harder to change, the documentation gaps widen because documenting a complex environment correctly is itself a complex activity.

This compounding dynamic means that the cost of deferred modernization investment is not linear. Every year of deferral makes the next year more expensive — both the cost of the deferral itself and the cost of the eventual modernization work. Organizations that invest early in architectural capability accumulate its benefits through compounding in the same way. Each improvement in architectural clarity makes the next improvement cheaper. Each increase in deployment frequency makes the next increase easier. The compounding works in both directions, and the organizations that understand this — that treat modernization investment as a compounding capability investment rather than a recurring cost — consistently outperform those that do not over the long run.

CHAPTER 4

Why Modernization Programs Fall Short

The five structural patterns that undermine modernization efforts — and what they reveal about the organizational capability required to succeed

Every organization that has invested significantly in software modernization has a story about a program that delivered less than expected. Sometimes the story involves a high-profile failure: a program that was cancelled after years of investment, or that was delivered at such a cost overrun that its business case was retroactively untenable. More often, the story is quieter: a program that technically delivered what it committed to but didn't produce the durable architectural improvement that motivated it, leaving the organization facing the same pressures again a few years later.

These outcomes are common enough, and consistent enough across industries and institutional contexts, to warrant serious examination. The patterns that produce them are not primarily failures of technology, execution capability, or organizational commitment. They are structural failures — rooted in how modernization has been conceptualized and organized, in assumptions that are embedded so deeply in planning frameworks that they are rarely questioned.

Understanding these patterns is not about assigning responsibility for past failures. It is about developing the diagnostic capability to recognize them in your own organization — and to build the Modernization Intelligence that allows you to address them rather than repeat them.

Pattern one — the program model

The program is the organizational unit through which most institutions manage large, complex initiatives. It has a defined scope, an assigned leadership team, a budget, a timeline, and a completion criterion. Programs are well-suited to many categories of organizational work. They are a poor fit for modernization.

The fundamental mismatch is between the bounded nature of a program and the unbounded nature of modernization. Programs end. Modernization doesn't. Software environments require continuous evolution — not because technology teams prefer to keep working, but because the demands on those environments change continuously. Regulatory requirements shift. Technology evolves. Operational needs grow. Strategic priorities change. An architecture that adequately serves today's demands will not adequately serve the demands of three years from now without active development.

An organization that modernizes its environment through a program and then redirects investment to other priorities is not completing its modernization work. It is purchasing a period of reduced architectural pressure — a few years, typically, before the gap between architectural condition and operational demands reopens enough to generate the pressure for the next program. This is the cycle that characterizes most institutions' relationship with modernization, and it is expensive, inefficient, and strategically limiting.

Programs also create incentive structures that are poorly aligned with the goals of modernization. Program leaders are accountable to program commitments — scope, schedule, budget. These commitments are made in advance of execution, under conditions of incomplete information about the environment and its dependencies. When the actual complexity of the environment exceeds the assumed complexity — as it reliably does — the program faces pressure to simplify scope, defer difficult dependencies, and declare completion at a point that satisfies the formal commitments without achieving the underlying architectural objectives.

These are rational responses to program incentives, not failures of character. But they produce a systematic pattern in which modernization programs deliver less architectural improvement than the investment in them would warrant — and in which the hardest and most important work is consistently deferred to the next program cycle.

Pattern two — replacement as the default strategy

The second structural failure pattern is the tendency to default to wholesale replacement as the modernization strategy for legacy systems. The appeal is understandable: starting fresh with modern technology, building to current requirements, without the constraints imposed by decades of accumulated complexity. The problem is that wholesale replacement is among the highest-risk strategies available and the one that most consistently underdelivers relative to expectations.

The core risk in replacement is what practitioners sometimes call the discovery problem: the gap between what replacement planners believe they are replacing and what they are actually replacing. Legacy systems in mature environments carry operational knowledge — business rules, edge cases, behavioral contracts with other systems — that is not fully visible from the outside and is not fully captured in any documentation. The only complete specification of what a legacy system does is the system itself.

Replacement programs that do not invest adequately in understanding what they are replacing consistently encounter this gap in the late stages of implementation — when the new system is deployed into production and begins to encounter cases that it handles incorrectly, integrations that it doesn't support as expected, or operational behaviors that downstream processes depend on that were not in any requirements document. The cost of discovering and addressing these gaps in production is dramatically higher than the cost of discovering them during design.

The replacement pattern also tends to underestimate the organizational complexity of cutover — the transition from the old system to the new one. In environments with dense dependencies, every system change has consequences for other systems, processes, and organizational workflows. Cutover from a major legacy system is not an event; it is a transition that requires parallel operation, progressive migration, careful validation, and organizational change management that extends over months or years. Programs that plan for a clean cutover consistently encounter a messy one.

None of this means that legacy systems should never be replaced. Sometimes replacement is genuinely the right strategy. The point is that it should be chosen based on an honest assessment of the full scope of what replacement requires — not assumed to be the default approach because it is conceptually simpler than the alternatives.

Pattern three — governance that cannot hold

The third failure pattern operates over longer timescales than the first two. Programs that begin with strong executive sponsorship and clear strategic rationale frequently find, several years in, that the governance structures supporting them cannot maintain coherence through the organizational changes that occur over extended timescales.

Leadership transitions are the most visible disruption. An executive who sponsored and championed a modernization program may be replaced by someone with different priorities, different relationships with technology, or simply less context on why the architectural decisions made early in the program were the right ones. New leadership may reduce program scope, redirect investment, or reverse architectural decisions in ways that undermine the coherence of what has been built — not out of malice but out of legitimate organizational authority being exercised without the full context that informed the original decisions.

Budget cycle pressures are a subtler but more consistent governance challenge. Annual planning cycles create recurring moments at which modernization investment is vulnerable to reallocation toward initiatives with more immediate and visible returns. Modernization investment produces returns that are deferred and diffuse — reduced maintenance costs in the future, preserved strategic optionality, improved organizational adaptability. These are real returns, but they are difficult to defend against the immediate returns of redirecting the same investment toward a product launch, a market expansion, or a cost reduction initiative.

The governance challenge in modernization is distinctive and deserves to be designed for explicitly. How does the institution maintain architectural integrity, strategic alignment, and investment continuity across multi-year transformation timelines, through the leadership changes and budget pressures that will inevitably occur? This question is rarely given adequate attention in program design, and the consequences of that neglect tend to appear in the middle and later phases of transformation, when the original coalition has dispersed and the structures to sustain it were never built.

Pattern four — the discovery gap

The fourth failure pattern is the discovery gap: the difference between what was known about the environment before transformation work began and what was discovered during it. In virtually every significant modernization effort, the actual complexity of the environment exceeds the assumed complexity. Dependencies that were not in any documentation turn out to be load-bearing. Behavioral contracts between systems that were never formally specified turn out to be critical. Organizational processes that depend on specific system behaviors turn out to require more change management than anyone anticipated.

The discovery gap is not a surprise, in the sense that experienced practitioners expect it. What is surprising is how consistently it is underinvested in. The temptation to move quickly to visible transformation work — to start building, to start migrating, to start the activities that look like progress — is strong enough that discovery work is routinely compressed or skipped. And the cost of that compression is routinely paid in the implementation phase, in the form of rework, delays, and the operational disruptions that occur when changes encounter undiscovered dependencies.

The organizations that manage the discovery gap most effectively are those that have developed organizational practices and cultural norms that treat discovery as first-class modernization work — as valuable and important as any implementation activity. They invest in it systematically, they staff it with experienced practitioners who know how to find things that are not in the documentation, and they create governance structures that protect the time and resources allocated to it from the pressures to accelerate that transformation programs consistently generate.

Pattern five — the completion fallacy

The fifth and most pervasive structural failure pattern is the belief that modernization has a completion state — that there is a point at which the work is done, the architecture is modern, and the investment can be redirected. This belief is so deeply embedded in how most institutions think about modernization that it shapes virtually every aspect of how modernization is organized, funded, and governed.

The completion fallacy produces the cycle described at the beginning of this chapter. Invest in transformation, declare completion, redirect investment, watch architectural debt accumulate, recognize the problem, begin the next transformation. This cycle is not a failure of organizational will. It is the predictable consequence of applying a completion-oriented model to work that does not have a natural completion point.

Technology evolves. Regulatory requirements change. Strategic priorities shift. Operational demands grow. What constitutes an adequate architecture at one point in time will not constitute an adequate architecture indefinitely. The organization that achieves genuine architectural excellence today will face new architectural challenges in three years — not because it has done anything wrong, but because the environment in which it operates will have changed in ways that create new requirements for architectural adaptation.

The only organizational model that is adequate to this reality is one that treats modernization as a permanent function rather than a periodic program. This is what Modernization Intelligence looks like in practice: not a series of transformation programs, but a sustained organizational capability — staffed, funded, governed, and developed as a permanent part of how the institution manages its own technological infrastructure.

SELF-ASSESSMENT — THE FIVE FAILURE PATTERNS

The following table provides a structured approach to assessing which of the five failure patterns are most active in your organization. For each pattern, rate your organization's current exposure on a scale of 1 (low exposure) to 5 (high exposure), and note the specific evidence that informs your rating.

Pattern	What to look for	Your exposure (1–5)	Key evidence
Program model	Modernization organized as		

	bounded projects; no permanent function; investment discontinued between programs		
Replacement default	Legacy systems routinely targeted for wholesale replacement; discovery work underinvested; cutover treated as an event		
Governance failure	Leadership transitions have reversed or diluted architectural decisions; annual planning cycles create vulnerability to investment reallocation		
Discovery gap	Significant undiscovered dependencies routinely found during implementation; transformation timelines regularly extended by		

	unexpected complexity		
Completion fallacy	Modernization programs declared complete; investment redirected; architectural debt re-accumulates between programs		

What these patterns share

Looking across the five patterns, a common thread emerges. Each pattern is a manifestation of the same underlying organizational condition: treating modernization as an episodic activity — something the organization does periodically in response to accumulated pressure — rather than as a continuous organizational capability.

The program model is the organizational structure of episodic activity. The replacement default is the strategy of episodic activity — doing something dramatic and definitive rather than something continuous and incremental. Governance failure is what happens when governance structures are designed for episodic programs rather than for continuous functions. The discovery gap is the cost of compressing discovery to fit the timeline of an episodic program. The completion fallacy is the mindset of episodic activity — the belief that there is an ending.

Modernization Intelligence is the antidote to the episodic model. It is the organizational capability that allows modernization to proceed as a continuous, managed, and increasingly effective institutional function. The following chapters work through what it means to build that capability, dimension by dimension.

LEADERSHIP NOTE — HAVING A DIFFERENT CONVERSATION

If the five patterns described in this chapter are recognizable in your organization, the most valuable thing this chapter can offer is not a diagnosis but a reframing for the leadership conversation. The patterns are not failures of the people involved — they are structural failures that produce predictable outcomes regardless of who is running the programs.

The conversation worth having at the leadership level is not 'how do we execute our next modernization program better?' It is 'what would it mean for us to develop a permanent modernization capability — and what would it require in terms of organizational structure, investment model, governance design, and leadership commitment?'

That conversation is harder than the program conversation. It requires a longer time horizon, a different investment framework, and a different kind of leadership engagement. But it is the right conversation, and Chapter Fourteen provides the practical framework for taking it from discussion to organizational design.

END OF PART ONE

Part One has established the foundational case. Software architecture has become strategic infrastructure. The real condition of modern software environments is more complex than planning frameworks typically acknowledge. Architectural friction imposes real, estimable, and compounding economic and strategic costs. And the traditional organizational model for addressing those costs — episodic transformation programs organized around the fiction of completion — has a structural failure mode that repeats regardless of who is running the programs.

Part Two builds on this foundation. It introduces the Modernization Intelligence framework and works through each of its five dimensions in depth — not as concepts, but as organizational capabilities that must be built, with specific guidance for how to build them.

Before moving to Part Two, the diagnostic tools embedded in this section are worth working through with your leadership team. The environmental clarity assessment in Chapter Two, the architectural friction cost framework in Chapter Three, and the failure pattern self-assessment in Chapter Four together provide a picture of where your organization currently stands and what the most important near-term investments are. That picture is the starting point for the work that follows.

PART TWO

The Modernization Intelligence Framework

The five dimensions of Modernization Intelligence — what each one means, how it works in practice, and the specific organizational capabilities required to build and sustain it.

CHAPTER 5

Introducing Modernization Intelligence

The framework defined — how the five dimensions interact, what it means to build them as an integrated system, and how to assess where to begin

Part One established the case for a different approach to modernization. It described the structural reality of modern software environments — the permanent hybrid condition, the embedded institutional knowledge in legacy systems, the density of accumulated dependencies. It described what architectural friction actually costs, in economic and strategic terms. And it identified the five structural patterns that have caused traditional modernization programs to fall short.

Part Two builds what Part One makes necessary: a framework for an organizational capability that addresses each of these structural challenges in a durable and principled way. That framework is Modernization Intelligence.

This chapter introduces the framework as a whole — its definition, its five dimensions, and the logic of how those dimensions work together as an integrated system. The chapters that follow each take one dimension in depth, working through the specific practices, tools, and governance structures that building that dimension requires. By the end of Part Two, you will have a complete picture of what Modernization Intelligence looks like in a fully developed organization, and a map for how to build it in your own.

The definition and its implications

Modernization Intelligence is the institutional capability that determines whether an organization can evolve its software environment without losing strategic momentum.

Each element of this definition is deliberate. It is an institutional capability — something the organization becomes able to do reliably, not something it does once. It determines — it is a primary variable, not a supporting one. Whether an organization can evolve its software environment — evolution, not replacement or transformation. Without losing strategic momentum — the constraint that makes it demanding. Most organizations can evolve their environments eventually. The ones that do it without losing the ability to pursue their strategic agenda while doing so are the ones that have built Modernization Intelligence.

Framing modernization as a capability rather than an activity has significant organizational implications. Capabilities are built and maintained. They are staffed, funded, and governed as permanent functions. They are evaluated on the quality of their outputs over time, not on the completion of specific deliverables. They improve with experience — each cycle of work builds the organizational learning that makes subsequent cycles more effective. These characteristics are exactly what sustained architectural evolution requires, and they are exactly what the program model of modernization fails to provide.

The capability framing also changes what success looks like. A successful modernization program is one that delivers its defined scope on time and within budget. A successful Modernization Intelligence capability is one that allows the organization to sustain architectural improvement continuously, at the pace that operational and strategic demands require, without the crises, overruns, and disruptions that characterize episodic approaches. These definitions require different organizational designs to achieve.

The five dimensions

Modernization Intelligence is composed of five integrated dimensions. They are not sequential phases. They are simultaneous, mutually reinforcing organizational capabilities that must operate together as a system. Understanding each dimension individually is necessary but not sufficient — the full value of the framework is realized only when all five are functioning and feeding one another.

Architectural awareness

Architectural awareness is the sustained organizational capability to understand the real state of the software environment — what exists, how it connects, what it depends on, and what the consequences of changing any part of it would be. It is the information foundation on which every other dimension depends. Without it, transformation sequencing is guesswork, execution discipline is working blind, and governance alignment is making decisions without adequate information.

Architectural awareness is distinguished from architectural documentation by its currency and operational character. Documentation describes how systems were designed. Architectural awareness describes how they actually function — including the implicit behaviors, undocumented dependencies, and organizational couplings that documentation almost never captures. Maintaining it requires ongoing investment, not periodic documentation efforts.

Transformation sequencing

Transformation sequencing is the capability to determine the order in which modernization work should proceed — to navigate the dependency landscape in ways that enable change without causing systemic disruption. It is the strategic planning function of modernization: translating architectural understanding into prioritized, executable transformation plans.

Good sequencing requires understanding which changes enable other changes, which dependencies must be resolved before subsequent work can proceed, and which changes carry operational risks that must be managed through specific sequencing decisions. Organizations with mature sequencing capability build explicit models of their transformation landscape — dependency maps, capability matrices, risk profiles — that allow sequencing decisions to be made analytically.

Execution discipline

Execution discipline is the operational capability to implement modernization work reliably within live environments. It encompasses the engineering practices, delivery patterns, and risk management approaches that allow significant changes to operational systems to be made without causing unacceptable disruption. In the modernization context, execution discipline is particularly demanding because the systems being changed are almost always supporting active operations.

Governance alignment

Governance alignment is the capability to maintain the connection between modernization work and institutional strategy across the multi-year timelines that architectural evolution requires. It addresses the structural challenge that has undermined more modernization programs than any other: the tendency for the governance structures, leadership commitments, and strategic rationale that initiated a transformation effort to erode over time as organizational context changes.

Continuous evolution

Continuous evolution is the fifth dimension and the one that most fundamentally distinguishes Modernization Intelligence from traditional modernization approaches. It is the organizational commitment to treat architectural development as a permanent function — to staff, fund, and govern it as an ongoing institutional responsibility rather than as a periodic project. When the other four dimensions are functioning well, continuous evolution is what results.

How the dimensions interact

The five dimensions form a system in which the outputs of each become inputs to the others. Architectural awareness feeds transformation sequencing: you cannot sequence intelligently what you do not understand. Transformation sequencing feeds execution discipline: you cannot execute with confidence what has not been thoughtfully sequenced. Execution discipline feeds continuous evolution: you cannot evolve continuously what you cannot execute reliably. Continuous evolution feeds architectural awareness: each cycle of work generates new knowledge that should improve subsequent cycles.

Governance alignment is the integrating force that holds all four together: it ensures that awareness activities are resourced, that sequencing decisions remain connected to strategic priorities, that execution is held accountable to both operational and architectural objectives, and that the continuous evolution commitment is protected from the organizational pressures that will otherwise erode it.

> *An organization with strong architectural awareness and weak governance will understand its problems clearly but be unable to sustain the investment required to address them. An organization with strong governance and weak architectural awareness will govern well on incomplete information. Both patterns are common; neither produces durable results.*

Where to begin

No organization builds all five dimensions simultaneously from scratch. Most organizations fall into one of four starting positions, determined by two variables: the clarity of their architectural understanding and the strength of their modernization governance.

Low clarity and weak governance: start with architectural awareness — Chapter Six. Reasonable clarity but weak governance: start with governance alignment — Chapter Nine. Weak clarity but reasonable governance: use the governance structures to commission and protect discovery investment — Chapter Six. Both reasonable: invest in transformation sequencing and execution discipline — Chapters Seven and Eight.

DIAGNOSTIC — WHERE DOES YOUR ORGANIZATION STAND?

Rate your organization on each of the two variables below, 1 (early stage) to 5 (mature).

Architectural clarity: Does your organization have a current, accurate understanding of your real software environment — systems, dependencies, operational behaviors, and integration complexity? Score 1 if you have only high-level diagrams; 5 if you have systematic, continuously maintained architectural intelligence trusted in decision-making.

Modernization governance: Do you have governance structures — decision rights, accountability mechanisms, executive engagement, funding models — that can maintain modernization investment across multi-year timelines? Score 1 if modernization is governed ad hoc within programs; 5 if you have a permanent governance function with operational accountability.

Clarity score 3 or below: begin with Chapter Six. Clarity above 3 and governance 3 or below: begin with Chapter Nine. Both above 3: read Chapters Seven and Eight in sequence, then return to Nine and Ten.

The maturity trajectory

Building Modernization Intelligence unfolds over years and requires sustained investment at every stage. The trajectory moves through three broad stages. In the first, the organization is building foundations: establishing awareness practices, creating governance structures, developing sequencing and execution capability. Returns are not yet visible — the investment is in capability infrastructure. In the second stage, foundations are operating and the organization is executing transformation work under the Modernization Intelligence discipline. Architectural improvement becomes visible and measurable. In the third stage, Modernization Intelligence has become an institutional habit. The organization is no longer talking about modernization as a strategic priority because it is no longer a crisis. It is simply how the institution manages its technological environment.

CHAPTER 6

Building Architectural Awareness

How to establish and maintain a continuously current, operationally accurate understanding of your software environment — the information foundation on which all modernization work depends

---

Architectural awareness is the most foundational of the five dimensions, and the most consistently underinvested. Organizations routinely begin transformation programs with architectural documentation that is years out of date, that covers only formally recognized systems while missing the shadow IT and implicit couplings that carry significant operational load, and that describes how systems were designed rather than how they currently behave. Building transformation plans on this foundation is the organizational equivalent of planning a renovation without understanding what is behind the walls.

This chapter provides a practical guide to building architectural awareness as an ongoing organizational capability — not as a one-time documentation effort but as a sustained practice that keeps the organization's understanding of its environment current, accurate, and operationally useful.

What architectural awareness is not

Architectural awareness is not an architecture diagram. Diagrams are representations of architectural decisions at a point in time, created during system design and updated occasionally, that gradually drift from the reality of the running environment. Architectural awareness is not a CMDB or asset inventory — those track what you have, not how what you have works. And architectural awareness is not the tacit knowledge of experienced individuals — valuable but fragile, concentrated in people who may leave and cannot be systematically applied to decision-making without organizational mechanisms.

Architectural awareness is a continuously maintained, organizationally shared, queryable body of knowledge about the real state of the software environment. It is built through deliberate practices, maintained through organizational discipline, and applied through governance mechanisms that connect it to modernization decisions.

The three components

Systems inventory

The systems inventory is a current, accurate understanding of what software systems exist in the environment and what each does. The challenge is scope. The formal enterprise systems register is never a complete picture — every mature institution has substantial shadow IT: tools built or adopted by business units without formal IT involvement, spreadsheet-based processes that carry operational load, locally maintained scripts, vendor-provided tools adopted outside procurement. An effective inventory requires active discovery across business units and engagement with the people who actually perform the work.

> **PRACTITIONER NOTE — CONDUCTING A SYSTEMS INVENTORY**
>
> A systems inventory useful for modernization planning requires three parallel discovery tracks.
>
> Technical discovery uses automated scanning — network discovery, software composition analysis, cloud asset inventory, API gateway logs — to identify running systems. Good at finding unknown systems; not good at telling you what they do or how they connect at the business process level.
>
> Process mapping engages operational teams. For each significant process, ask: what systems does this touch, in what

order, and what would happen if each were unavailable for a day? This surfaces operational significance and reveals systems technical scanning misses.
Organizational archaeology reviews change history — deployment logs, change records, infrastructure invoices, vendor contracts — revealing systems no longer actively used but still running, or actively used but not in any formal register.
The output is not a comprehensive database but a structured, categorized list with enough information about each system to support modernization planning: what it does, who owns it, its operational significance, and what is known about its integrations.

Dependency mapping

Dependency mapping goes beyond systems inventory to understand how systems connect — what they exchange, what they rely on in each other's behavior, and what would break if specific components were changed. Effective dependency mapping operates at three levels.

Surface-level dependencies are formally documented integrations: APIs described in specifications, data feeds in integration catalogues, batch transfers in workflow management systems. These are the starting point — representing perhaps fifty to sixty percent of actual coupling in most environments.

Behavioral dependencies are implicit couplings: timing assumptions a downstream system relies on from upstream, format dependencies a consuming system depends on beyond what the API specification requires, performance dependencies based on undocumented response time assumptions. Invisible until violated — the primary source of surprise in modernization execution.

Organizational dependencies are business processes and operational workflows designed around specific system behaviors: a reconciliation process that runs because a system produces a weekly summary at a specific time, an escalation workflow that depends on a CRM field populated by a nightly batch. Entirely invisible to technical analysis but causing operational disruption when changes are made without accounting for them.

Operational behavior documentation

The third component is the most qualitative and hardest to systematize: documentation of how systems actually behave in production. This includes the business logic embedded in system behavior, the edge cases handled by code rather than documented rules, the operational quirks experienced operators compensate for, and the failure modes addressed over the system's operational life. This knowledge is almost always tacit — held by individuals, created through years of operational experience. The organizational practice required is structured knowledge capture: deliberate, recurring conversations with experienced operators in which tacit knowledge is surfaced and documented in forms that can be shared and preserved.

Maintaining awareness over time

The most common failure mode in architectural awareness is not building it initially — it is allowing it to decay. The environment changes; documentation does not keep pace. Three mechanisms work together to prevent this.

Change-triggered updates: every significant change to the environment should trigger an update to the architectural knowledge base. Embedding this into the change management process — making documentation updates part of the deployment definition of done — is the most reliable mechanism.

Periodic verification: a quarterly or semi-annual cycle in which a sample of systems and integrations are audited against the knowledge base catches the drift that change-triggered processes miss.

Incident-driven learning: when an incident surfaces a dependency or behavior not in the knowledge base, that gap should be documented immediately. Incidents are the most reliable signal of architectural knowledge gaps, and building a systematic practice of extracting architectural knowledge from incident retrospectives converts operational failures into organizational learning.

TOOL — ARCHITECTURAL AWARENESS MATURITY ASSESSMENT

Rate each statement 1 (not true) to 4 (consistently true).

Systems inventory: We have a current, accurate inventory of all production systems, including shadow IT and locally maintained tools that carry operational load.

Dependency mapping: We have documented dependencies between core systems at sufficient depth to make confident sequencing decisions about changes to any of them.

Behavioral knowledge: The operational behaviors of core systems — implicit dependencies and embedded business logic — are documented and accessible to the teams that need them.

Platform currency: Our architectural knowledge base is updated when significant changes are made, and we have mechanisms to detect and correct drift.

Decision utility: Our architectural knowledge is actively used in modernization planning and governance decisions, not just maintained as documentation.

Score 16-20: strong foundation. Score 10-15: significant gaps to address. Below 10: prioritize the systems inventory and dependency audit processes above before committing to major transformation work.

CHAPTER 7

Sequencing Transformation Intelligently

How to determine the order in which modernization work should proceed — navigating the dependency landscape to enable change without systemic disruption

---

If architectural awareness is the information foundation of Modernization Intelligence, transformation sequencing is its strategic brain. It translates architectural knowledge into prioritized, executable plans — answering the question every modernization leader faces: given everything we know about our environment, what should we work on first, and why?

This question is harder than it appears. Starting with the most visible legacy systems often means starting with the most complex and risky changes before the organizational capability for managing that complexity has been developed. Starting with the easiest changes can mean executing in an order that creates new dependencies or forecloses later options. Effective sequencing requires a systematic approach.

The principles of intelligent sequencing

Dependency first

The most important sequencing principle is dependency ordering: changes that must precede other changes should precede them. In a densely connected environment, almost every significant modernization change has dependencies. Building a dependency-ordered transformation plan means mapping these relationships explicitly and using them to determine sequence.

Dependency ordering often means doing significant foundational work before visible progress can be shown. Establishing a reliable integration platform before migrating applications to it. Instrumenting systems with observability before making significant changes to them. Documenting and testing behavioral contracts before attempting to change either side. This work does not show up as modernization progress in typical program reporting, but without it, subsequent progress is built on sand.

Risk calibration

Not all modernization changes carry equal risk. Sound sequencing accounts for this distribution — sequencing lower-risk changes earlier to build organizational confidence and capability, and to deliver early improvement that builds institutional support for subsequent higher-risk work. Risk calibration requires honest assessment across multiple dimensions: technical complexity, operational coupling, reversibility, and timing sensitivity.

Value acceleration

Within the constraints of dependency ordering and risk calibration, sequence changes to deliver operational value as early as possible. Early operational value builds organizational confidence and leadership commitment that sustains investment in subsequent phases. Map the specific operational improvements that modernization delivers to specific points in the transformation sequence, and prefer sequences that deliver high value early.

The sequencing toolkit

The dependency matrix

The dependency matrix is the core analytical tool for transformation sequencing — a structured representation of the relationships between modernization initiatives: which must precede others, which can proceed in parallel, and which must follow. The matrix analysis surfaces the natural phases of the transformation: groups of initiatives that can proceed in parallel, followed by groups whose preconditions have been satisfied by the previous phase.

Initiative	Depends on	Enables	Risk level
Integration platform	None	App migration wave 1, Data pipeline	High
Observability tooling	None	All subsequent changes	Medium
App migration wave 1	Integration platform, Observability	App migration wave 2	Medium
Data pipeline modernization	Integration platform	Analytics platform	High
App migration wave 2	Wave 1 complete	Legacy retirement	Medium
Legacy system retirement	Wave 2, Data pipeline complete	None	High

Example dependency matrix for a modernization program

The risk-value matrix

The risk-value matrix maps each modernization initiative on two dimensions: operational value and execution risk. High-value, low-risk changes are natural starting points. High-value, high-risk changes require careful preparation. Low-value changes, regardless of risk level, should be examined critically before being included — they consume organizational capacity that could be directed toward higher-value work.

The transformation roadmap

The transformation roadmap combines dependency matrix analysis and risk-value analysis with institutional strategic priorities and operational constraints. An effective roadmap is explicitly dependency-ordered with documented sequencing rationale; includes preparation activities as first-class deliverables; identifies operational improvements for each phase, not just technical deliverables; and is maintained as a living document updated as the environment changes and execution generates new information.

Keeping sequencing current

Treating the transformation roadmap as a static plan is a common and costly failure. Sequencing should be revisited quarterly at minimum, and immediately when significant changes occur in the environment, strategic context, or execution experience. The questions to ask: has the dependency landscape changed? Has execution revealed dependencies not in the original plan? Have strategic priorities shifted? Has organizational risk tolerance changed? Organizations that treat sequencing as a continuous strategic function consistently make better transformation decisions and encounter fewer surprises.

Common sequencing mistakes

Skipping foundations is the most consequential mistake: moving directly to visible transformation work without establishing the integration, observability, and architectural knowledge foundations that subsequent work depends on. The cost surfaces reliably in the execution phase, in forms more expensive than the investment in foundations would have been.

Parallel execution without dependency analysis executes multiple initiatives simultaneously without adequately understanding the dependencies between them. Some parallelism is appropriate, but in densely coupled environments, unanalyzed parallelism creates interference risks that are expensive and difficult to unwind.

Business-priority sequencing without technical ordering sequences work based purely on business value without adequate consideration of technical dependencies. The most strategically important initiative may not be the right thing to execute first if it depends on foundational changes not yet made.

TOOL — SEQUENCING DECISION CHECKLIST

Before committing to a transformation sequence for any significant initiative, work through the following. Each question that cannot be answered with confidence represents a gap to address before proceeding.

Dependency readiness: Have all preceding initiatives been completed or scheduled to complete before this one begins? Have the behavioral contracts between this system and its dependencies been documented and tested?

Risk assessment: Has the execution risk been explicitly assessed across technical complexity, operational coupling, reversibility, and timing sensitivity? Are mitigation strategies in place?

Foundation readiness: Is observability tooling in place to monitor this change in production? Is the rollback plan documented and tested? Is the parallel operation strategy defined?

Organizational readiness: Does the execution team have the required skills? Have operational teams whose workflows will be affected been engaged? Is the governance body aware of this change and its risk profile?

Strategic alignment: Is the business case current? Have the strategic priorities this initiative serves been confirmed as still active? Is the expected value still achievable given any contextual changes since the roadmap was built?

CHAPTER 8

Executing in Live Environments

The engineering practices, delivery patterns, and risk management approaches that allow significant modernization changes to be made without causing unacceptable operational disruption

---

Execution discipline is where the strategic and analytical work of Modernization Intelligence meets operational reality. It determines whether sound architectural decisions — grounded in genuine awareness and carefully sequenced — can be translated into actual changes to live systems without the kind of disruption that undermines organizational confidence and derails modernization programs.

The challenge of execution in the modernization context is distinctive. The systems being changed are almost always carrying active operational load. The dependencies being navigated are live. The consequences of execution failures are immediate and often significant. This chapter covers the specific engineering practices, delivery patterns, and organizational disciplines that constitute execution discipline in this context.

The incremental delivery imperative

The single most important execution discipline principle in modernization is incrementalism: making changes in the smallest viable units that can be validated in production before further commitment. This runs counter to the instincts of many modernization programs — the instinct to make a clean break, to execute a definitive migration, to complete a full replacement before production exposure.

The case for incrementalism is grounded in the structural realities of Chapter Two. Mature environments contain dependencies, behavioral contracts, and operational behaviors that cannot be fully discovered in advance. Every significant modernization change will encounter surprises. The question is whether the organization encounters them in a controlled way, with limited operational impact, or in a crisis, when a large-scale change has already been committed. Incremental delivery structures the exposure to surprises: each increment is small enough that its consequences are bounded and reversible, and each generates real-world validation data that improves the accuracy of the plan for subsequent increments.

Core execution practices

Feature toggles and dark launches

Feature toggles allow new capabilities or changed behaviors to be deployed to production without being activated — the new code runs in the real environment under real operational conditions without the change being live. This provides a critical validation layer between development and full production activation.

Dark launches extend this principle: the new capability runs in production alongside the old one, processing real requests and generating real outputs, but those outputs are compared to the existing system's outputs rather than used authoritatively. For complex legacy replacements, dark launch validation is one of the most powerful tools for discovering behavioral differences before they cause production failures.

Parallel operation strategies

Parallel operation — running old and new systems simultaneously during transition — allows the new system to be validated under production conditions while the old system remains authoritative. The parallel operation period should be used actively: systematically comparing the outputs of old and new systems across a representative sample of scenarios, with particular attention to edge cases and boundary conditions most likely to surface behavioral differences. The conditions under which cutover will occur should be explicitly defined before the parallel operation period begins, not determined ad hoc when organizational pressure to complete the migration builds.

Strangler fig architecture

The strangler fig pattern incrementally replaces legacy functionality by building new capabilities alongside existing ones. New requests are routed to the new implementation while old requests continue to be served by the legacy system, allowing migration to proceed incrementally as new capabilities are verified. This avoids the big-bang cutover risk — in a strangler fig approach, there is no single cutover moment. Applying the pattern requires investment in routing and abstraction infrastructure that should be established early in any program involving significant legacy system work.

Comprehensive observability

Observability — the ability to understand internal system state from external outputs — is a prerequisite for confident modernization execution. Without it, the organization cannot tell whether a change has affected system behavior in unexpected ways, whether performance has changed, or whether error rates have increased in ways that should trigger rollback. Observability requires three components: logging for detailed event records, metrics for aggregate behavior over time, and tracing to connect request execution across multiple systems. Establishing observability infrastructure before executing significant modernization changes is non-negotiable.

Rollback planning

Every significant modernization change should have a documented, tested rollback plan before execution. The rollback plan specifies exactly how the change will be reversed if it causes unacceptable operational impact: what actions are required, in what order, by whom, and within what time window. Building a rollback plan forces explicit consideration of what could go wrong, identifies data migration and state management challenges that rollback would involve, and creates organizational readiness to execute rollback quickly and confidently. The rollback plan should be tested in a staging environment before the change is executed in production. The first time a rollback plan is executed should never be in a production incident.

Execution team structure and readiness

Effective modernization execution teams combine technical depth with architectural context: engineers who understand the systems being changed at a code level, architects who understand the dependency landscape and strategic goals, and operational specialists who understand how the change will affect the people and processes that depend on the systems. Execution readiness should be assessed explicitly before each significant change across four dimensions: technical readiness (complete, tested, reviewed), operational readiness (affected teams prepared and informed), governance readiness (appropriate approvals obtained), and rollback readiness (plan documented, tested, and understood by everyone involved).

TOOL — EXECUTION READINESS CHECKLIST

Complete this checklist before committing any significant modernization change to production. A 'no' answer is a signal to pause and address the gap before proceeding.

Technical readiness: Change reviewed by at least two engineers with relevant expertise. All automated tests pass including dependency regression tests. Performance characteristics validated in staging. Observability instrumentation in place and verified.

Dependency readiness: All upstream dependencies in their expected state. Downstream consumers notified and have confirmed readiness. Behavioral contracts between changed system and dependencies validated.

Operational readiness: Teams operating and supporting affected systems understand the change and its expected effects. Support runbook for the change period distributed. Out-of-hours contacts confirmed.

Rollback readiness: Rollback plan documented and reviewed by the execution team. Rollback plan rehearsed in staging. Rollback trigger conditions explicitly defined and understood by everyone involved. Data state management for rollback tested.

Governance readiness: Change reviewed and approved by the appropriate governance body. Business owner of affected systems confirmed awareness and readiness. Communication plan executed.

CHAPTER 9

Governing Modernization Across Time

How to build governance structures that maintain strategic coherence, executive engagement, and investment continuity across the multi-year timelines that architectural evolution requires

---

Of the five dimensions of Modernization Intelligence, governance alignment is the one most consistently designed inadequately. Organizations invest in architectural awareness, build sequencing capability, and develop execution discipline — and then find that without governance structures adequate to the timescales involved, those investments fail to produce durable results. Sequencing plans are overridden by leadership decisions made without architectural context. Execution is accelerated beyond safe limits by schedule pressures that governance is not equipped to manage. Investment is redirected when budget cycles create opportunities to reallocate it toward initiatives with more immediately visible returns.

This chapter addresses the organizational design of modernization governance: what makes it different from project or operational governance, what structures are required, how to design for your specific context, and how to build it incrementally from wherever you are starting.

What makes modernization governance different

Three structural requirements distinguish modernization governance from other governance contexts. First, temporal span: meaningful architectural evolution unfolds over multi-year timelines, and the governance structures that support it must maintain coherence through the leadership transitions, budget cycles, and organizational changes that will occur over those timelines. Standard project governance is designed for programs of one to three years. Modernization governance must function effectively over periods of five to ten years or more.

Second, cross-domain scope: modernization decisions involve the intersection of technical, operational, regulatory, financial, and strategic considerations that span organizational boundaries. Governance that operates within a single domain is inadequate. Effective modernization governance must bring together the technical credibility to understand architectural choices, the business authority to connect them to strategic priorities, the financial perspective to evaluate investment trade-offs, and the risk judgment to assess implications.

Third, decision continuity: architectural decisions made early in a modernization program create commitments that constrain choices for years. When governance structures change, those commitments need to be carried forward coherently. This requires explicit mechanisms for transferring architectural context across governance transitions — not just the decisions but the reasoning behind them.

The three governance functions

Decision alignment

Decision alignment connects modernization decisions to institutional strategy — ensuring that the architectural investments being made are the ones most likely to enable the strategic capabilities the institution is working to build. The governance body responsible for this function must have genuine authority: the ability to make consequential decisions about modernization priorities, investment levels, and sequencing choices, not just to review and advise. The cadence should be quarterly at minimum, with a continuous connection to the strategic planning process between meetings.

Architectural oversight

Architectural oversight maintains the integrity of architectural decisions across distributed modernization execution. Without it, individual team decisions will produce local optimization at the cost of global coherence — new forms of the fragmentation that modernization was intended to address. Effective oversight requires both standards (the architectural guardrails within which teams make decisions) and judgment (the mechanism for evaluating decisions that fall outside standards and for updating standards when context changes). The oversight function must operate at the speed of execution without creating bottlenecks — focusing on decisions that genuinely require cross-cutting perspective, not approving every technical choice.

Transformation accountability

Transformation accountability tracks progress against modernization objectives and creates the organizational consequences — corrective, not punitive — that sustain investment and attention over time. Effective accountability requires outcome metrics, not delivery metrics. Technical debt trajectory: is the total identified stock declining? Change velocity: how quickly can changes be implemented from requirement identification to deployment? Disruption rate: are operational incidents attributable to architectural friction declining? Strategic capability enablement: what new capabilities has modernization enabled? A program that delivers all its planned milestones but leaves architectural condition unchanged has not succeeded at modernization.

Designing governance for your context

Centralization versus federation

The fundamental governance design choice is the degree of centralization: how much authority sits in a central body versus how much is delegated to business units or domains. Highly centralized governance provides coherence and consistent standards but can become a bottleneck. Highly federated governance enables autonomy but risks incoherence. Most large institutions find the most effective model on a federated-with-coherence spectrum: significant autonomy for domain-level decisions within architectural standards established and enforced centrally. The calibration challenge is how prescriptive the central standards are — prescriptive enough to prevent fragmentation, flexible enough to allow domain-appropriate decisions.

Governance cadence

For most organizations, a quarterly strategic governance cadence — focused on investment priorities, architectural direction, and strategic alignment — paired with a monthly operational cadence — focused on execution progress, risk management, and issue resolution — provides an appropriate balance. The cadence should be frequent enough to stay connected to evolving execution work and course-correct drift, but not so frequent that it consumes the organizational energy required for actual transformation.

Leadership engagement depth

The most critical governance design question is depth of executive engagement. Nominal sponsorship is insufficient for governance that must maintain coherence across multi-year timelines. Effective modernization governance requires executives who understand the architectural choices being made well enough to defend them when challenged, evaluate proposed changes against their strategic rationale, and maintain investment commitments through competing pressures. Building this depth requires deliberate investment in executive education on architectural matters — not to make executives into technical experts but to give them sufficient fluency to participate meaningfully in governance conversations.

TOOL — MODERNIZATION GOVERNANCE HEALTH CHECK

Use these questions annually to identify governance gaps that should be addressed.

Decision authority: Does the governance body have genuine authority to make consequential decisions about priorities, investment, and sequencing — or does it function primarily as a review and advisory body?
Strategic connection: Are modernization investment decisions explicitly connected to strategic priorities, with documented rationale linking architectural choices to strategic outcomes?
Continuity mechanisms: When leadership changes occur, is there a reliable mechanism for transferring architectural context — not just decisions but the reasoning behind them?
Outcome tracking: Are modernization outcomes tracked through metrics that measure architectural improvement, not just activity and delivery?
Accountability consequence: When modernization work drifts from its strategic rationale or fails to produce expected outcomes, are there governance consequences that get work back on track?
Protection from reallocation: Does the governance model include mechanisms that protect core modernization investment from being reallocated during budget cycles?

CHAPTER 10

Making Modernization Continuous

How to transition from episodic transformation programs to a permanent organizational function — the staffing models, funding structures, and institutional habits that sustain continuous architectural evolution

---

The preceding four chapters have worked through the operational dimensions of Modernization Intelligence: the awareness, sequencing, execution, and governance capabilities that allow modernization to be done well. This final chapter of Part Two addresses the organizational dimension that makes those capabilities permanent: continuous evolution.

Continuous evolution is the commitment to treat architectural development as an ongoing institutional function. It is the organizational design that ensures the other four dimensions are not just built but sustained — that architectural awareness is maintained rather than decaying, that sequencing decisions are kept current, that execution capability develops continuously, and that governance structures maintain effectiveness through organizational change.

Building this permanence requires changes to how modernization is organized, staffed, funded, measured, and led. This chapter works through each with the specificity needed to actually make the transition.

From program to function

The most important organizational transition in building continuous evolution is from the program model to the function model. A program is a temporary construct with a completion criterion. When it ends, the team disbands and organizational attention moves elsewhere. A function is a permanent construct with ongoing accountabilities that persist indefinitely — how organizations manage the work that never ends: financial management, human resources, legal and compliance.

The transition from program to function is not a relabeling. It requires changes in how the work is scoped (ongoing improvement rather than defined deliverables), staffed (permanent roles rather than temporary project assignments), funded (operational budget rather than capital appropriation), governed (continuous oversight rather than program reporting), and how success is defined (improvement in architectural condition over time rather than delivery of specific outputs).

Staffing the modernization function

The staffing model for a permanent modernization function differs from that for a program. Programs aggregate large teams for defined periods and then disband them. Functions need smaller, more stable teams with deep organizational knowledge that accumulates over time. The core modernization function team needs three essential capabilities: architectural intelligence (understanding and maintaining knowledge of the environment), strategic planning (translating that knowledge into sound transformation sequences), and execution leadership (leading transformation work reliably). In a small organization, three to five people may carry all three. In a large, complex institution, the core function may be larger — but its effectiveness derives from institutional knowledge and coordination capability, not headcount.

The talent profile is genuinely distinctive: deep technical capability, strategic judgment, organizational fluency, and communication skill. Finding all of this in a single individual is difficult. Building it in a team — through deliberate combination of complementary skills and a culture of continuous learning — is more practical and more resilient. When hiring for the modernization function, weigh demonstrated judgment and organizational effectiveness as heavily as technical expertise.

Funding the modernization function

How modernization is funded determines more about how it operates than almost any other organizational design decision. Capital project funding — approval as a capital appropriation for specific programs — produces program-centric behavior almost inevitably. Capital programs have completion dates. When the completion date arrives, the investment ends, regardless of organizational intent.

Operational budget funding — an ongoing operational budget that the function is accountable for spending effectively — is the model appropriate to a permanent function. It removes the artificial program endpoint. It enables investment in foundational capabilities — awareness infrastructure, execution tooling, team development — whose returns are realized over periods longer than any single program cycle. And it creates accountability for ongoing outcomes rather than specific deliverables.

The transition from capital to operational funding is often the hardest organizational change in building continuous evolution capability. The argument is straightforward: if modernization is genuinely a permanent function, funding it as a temporary project is a structural mismatch that produces dysfunction. The investment in making the funding model match the organizational reality is worth making.

Measuring continuous evolution

Measuring the effectiveness of a continuous evolution function requires metrics that reflect cumulative improvement in architectural condition over time. Four categories apply broadly:

Technical debt trajectory tracks the total identified stock of technical debt over time. When the modernization function can demonstrate that total identified technical debt is declining quarter over quarter, that is a meaningful indicator of functional effectiveness.

Change velocity measures how quickly changes can be made to the environment from requirement identification to production deployment. Improving change velocity is one of the primary operational benefits of architectural improvement: as legacy constraints are removed and integration complexity is reduced, the time required to implement changes decreases.

Disruption rate measures the frequency and severity of operational disruptions attributable to architectural friction — incidents from undocumented dependencies, integration failures, change-caused regressions. A declining disruption rate indicates improving architectural quality and execution discipline.

Strategic capability enablement tracks what new strategic capabilities modernization work has made possible — services that could not previously be offered, integrations that could not previously be supported, regulatory requirements that can now be met without manual workarounds. This is the measure that connects the modernization function most directly to institutional strategic value.

Building the institutional habits

Beyond organizational structure, funding, and measurement, continuous evolution requires institutional habits: the recurring practices and cultural norms that make architectural improvement a normal dimension of institutional technology management.

The most important is the regular retrospective: a structured, recurring examination of what modernization work has been done, what it produced, what was learned, and how that learning should affect subsequent work. The retrospective is the mechanism through which the flywheel model operates — each cycle generating the learning that makes subsequent cycles more effective. Organizations that skip or shortchange retrospectives run the flywheel without engaging the compounding mechanism.

The second critical habit is architectural debt recognition: explicitly identifying and documenting technical debt as it is created. When a pragmatic shortcut is taken, that debt should be documented immediately, sized, and added to the architectural debt register. Invisible debt is the kind that compounds most dangerously.

The third is continuous discovery: regularly examining parts of the environment that have not been the focus of recent modernization attention, specifically looking for the accumulation of complexity and debt that occurs in low-visibility corners of the architecture. The systems that cause the biggest modernization surprises are often not the ones everyone knows about — they are the ones nobody has looked at recently.

> *Continuous evolution is not achieved at a point in time. It is the result of institutional habits, developed and sustained over years, that make architectural improvement a normal dimension of how the organization manages itself.*

TOOL — CONTINUOUS EVOLUTION READINESS ASSESSMENT

Use this assessment to evaluate your organization's readiness to operate as a continuous evolution function rather than an episodic program executor.

Function structure: Does modernization have a permanent organizational home — a named function with a mandate, leadership, and ongoing accountabilities — or is it organized as a series of programs?
Funding model: Is the modernization function funded through an operational budget that persists across planning cycles, or through capital appropriations for specific programs?
Staffing continuity: Does the modernization function have a stable core team with accumulating institutional knowledge, or is the team assembled fresh for each program cycle?
Outcome measurement: Does the function track and report on indicators of architectural improvement — technical debt trajectory, change velocity, disruption rate — in addition to or instead of delivery metrics?
Learning practices: Does the function have regular retrospective practices that extract organizational learning from each cycle of work and apply it forward?
Executive continuity: Do the executives who sponsor the function have sufficient architectural context to maintain their engagement and commitment through normal organizational changes?

END OF PART TWO

Part Two has built the Modernization Intelligence framework from the ground up. Chapter Five defined the framework and the five dimensions, and described how they interact as an integrated system. Chapters Six through Ten worked through each dimension in depth — architectural awareness, transformation sequencing, execution discipline, governance alignment, and continuous evolution — providing the specific practices, tools, and organizational designs required to build each one.

The tools embedded throughout Part Two are designed to be applied directly. They are most useful when used together: a complete picture of Modernization Intelligence maturity in your organization, with a clear map of where the investment gaps are. Completing all five assessments before moving to Part Three will give you a grounded starting point for the diagnostic and implementation work that Part Three provides.

Part Three takes the framework into practice. It provides diagnostic tools for assessing your current maturity, guidance for identifying which modernization archetype describes your situation, practical guidance on integrating AI capabilities into the modernization function, and the organizational design guidance for building the modernization function itself — the chapter where the analytical work of Parts One and Two becomes the implementation work of your organization.

CHAPTER 9

Governing Modernization Across Time

What governance actually means in the modernization context, how to build the structures that sustain it, and how to protect it through the organizational changes that will inevitably test it

---

Governance is one of those words that means different things to different people depending on which part of an organization they sit in. To a program manager, governance is the approval process that slows things down. To a CFO, it is the control structure that protects investment. To a CTO, it is the mechanism that either enables good architectural decisions or prevents them. To a board member, it is the accountability framework that determines whether the organization's most significant investments are producing the returns they were intended to produce.

All of these framings contain something true. None of them, on its own, captures what governance needs to be in the modernization context. Before getting to how to build modernization governance, it is worth spending time on what it actually is — because the misunderstandings are consequential, and they produce governance designs that fail in predictable ways.

What governance actually means

At its most basic, governance is the system of structures, processes, and norms through which an organization makes decisions, allocates resources, and holds itself accountable for outcomes. Every organization has governance, whether it has designed it explicitly or not. The question is not whether governance exists but whether the governance that exists is adequate to the decisions it is supposed to support.

In the modernization context, governance is the system through which the organization answers four recurring questions. First: are we investing in the right architectural changes — the ones most likely to enable the strategic capabilities we are trying to build? Second: are the architectural decisions being made across the distributed execution of modernization work coherent with each other and with the direction the organization has chosen? Third: are we making progress — is the architecture actually improving, at the pace the institution requires? Fourth: when the answers to the first three questions are no, what do we do about it?

These are not technical questions. They are organizational questions. And the governance structures that answer them need to be organizational structures — not just technical review processes, and not just financial approval mechanisms. They need to bring together the perspectives required to answer these questions well: strategic, technical, financial, operational, and risk.

> *Governance is not what happens to modernization from the outside. It is the organizational intelligence that guides modernization from within. When it works well, it is invisible — decisions get made well, investment is sustained, and the work stays connected to institutional purpose. When it fails, everything downstream fails with it.*

Why modernization governance fails

Before designing modernization governance, it is worth understanding the most common ways that governance in this domain fails. Each failure mode reflects a structural flaw that good governance design can address — but only if the flaw is recognized.

Governance by exception

The most common failure mode is governance that only activates when something goes wrong. In this model, modernization work proceeds largely autonomously until a crisis — a missed milestone, a significant cost overrun, a production incident caused by a modernization change — triggers governance attention. The governance body convenes, investigates, intervenes, and then stands down until the next crisis.

This pattern produces bad outcomes for reasons that are structural rather than personal. Governance by exception means that the governance body is always operating in reactive mode — responding to failures rather than preventing them. It means that the accumulated architectural context required to make good decisions about complex trade-offs is never built, because the governance body does not maintain sufficient ongoing engagement to develop it. And it means that the organizational relationships between technical and non-technical leaders that effective modernization governance requires are never strengthened, because those leaders only interact when something has already gone wrong.

Governance by proxy

A second common failure mode is governance that is nominally present but operationally absent — where senior leaders are listed as sponsors or steering committee members but are not genuinely engaged in the decisions that matter. The real governance happens at lower levels of the organization, often within the IT function, without the cross-functional perspective and organizational authority that effective modernization governance requires.

Governance by proxy is particularly dangerous in the context of long-horizon investment decisions. When architectural choices that will constrain institutional options for five or ten years are being made by people who do not have the authority or the strategic perspective to make them well, the choices that get made will tend to reflect technical preferences rather than institutional priorities. And when budget cycles or leadership changes create pressure to redirect modernization investment, there is no governance structure with sufficient authority and commitment to protect it.

Governance without continuity

The third failure mode is governance structures that cannot maintain coherence through the organizational changes that occur over multi-year modernization timelines. A new CTO arrives and brings different architectural preferences. A new CFO questions the business case for investments committed by their predecessor. A new CEO reorganizes the technology function in ways that dissolve the governance structures that were in place. In each case, the institutional knowledge and commitment that had been built into the previous governance structure is lost, and the modernization program must either rebuild its governance foundation or proceed without one.

This failure mode is not primarily about personnel quality. The new leaders who disrupt established modernization governance are typically doing their jobs — bringing their own judgment, questioning inherited commitments, and organizing their functions in ways that make sense to them. The failure is structural: governance that was built around individual leaders rather than institutional roles, decision processes that carried reasoning in people's heads rather than in documented records, and commitment mechanisms that depended on specific relationships rather than on institutional structures.

The components of governance: a first-principles view

With these failure modes in mind, it is possible to describe what effective modernization governance needs to contain from first principles. There are five essential components, each addressing a specific governance requirement that the failure modes above make visible.

Decision authority

Effective governance requires clear decision authority: an explicit definition of who has the power to make which decisions about modernization investment, direction, and execution. Decision authority in modernization is more complex than in most other organizational domains because the decisions involved span multiple organizational functions and multiple levels of the hierarchy.

At the strategic level, decisions about the overall direction and investment level of modernization — which architectural goals to pursue, how much to invest, how to balance modernization investment against other institutional priorities — require authority at the executive level. These decisions affect the institution's strategic options over multi-year horizons and cannot be made well below the level at which those horizons are managed.

At the architectural level, decisions about the specific changes that will be made to the environment — which platforms, which integration patterns, which migration sequences — require authority that combines technical credibility with organizational legitimacy. This is typically the domain of a principal architect or architecture function, operating within strategic parameters set at the executive level.

At the execution level, decisions about how specific changes are implemented — delivery approach, timeline, resource allocation, risk management — require authority that sits with the teams doing the work, within architectural and strategic parameters established above. Micromanaging execution from governance bodies is a common error that produces bureaucratic friction without improving decision quality.

Clarity about which level owns which decisions — and the discipline to make decisions at the right level rather than escalating unnecessarily or delegating inappropriately — is one of the most important design choices in modernization governance.

Information flow

Governance bodies can only make good decisions if they receive good information. In modernization governance, the information challenge is significant: the people who have the deepest understanding of the architectural environment are typically not the people who sit on governance bodies, and the information that governance bodies typically receive — program status updates, milestone reports, budget utilization summaries — does not give them the architectural context they need to make consequential decisions well.

Effective modernization governance requires a deliberate investment in information translation: the organizational practice of taking complex architectural information and presenting it in forms that are accessible and decision-useful for non-technical governance participants. This is not about dumbing things down. It is about presenting the right information at the right level of abstraction to support the specific decisions that the governance body needs to make.

A governance body deciding whether to accelerate a major platform migration does not need to understand the technical details of the migration approach. It does need to understand: what is the operational risk profile of the migration? What strategic capabilities does it enable, and when? What happens if it is deferred? What would acceleration require in terms of investment and organizational capacity? Translating the architectural reality into these decision-relevant terms is a skill that modernization leaders need to develop and maintain.

Commitment mechanisms

Governance decisions are only as valuable as the organizational commitment that follows them. One of the most consistent failure patterns in modernization governance is the decision that is made and then not acted on: the investment that is approved but then gradually redirected, the architectural direction that is set and then quietly abandoned, the accountability consequence that is agreed and then not enforced.

Commitment mechanisms are the organizational structures that make governance decisions sticky — that convert decisions into durable organizational commitments that persist through the competing pressures that will arise. They include investment protection structures that make modernization funding difficult to redirect without a formal governance decision to do so. They include architectural decision records that document not just the decisions themselves but the reasoning behind them, making them robust to the leadership transitions that might otherwise lead to their reversal. And they include accountability cadences that regularly surface the question of whether previous commitments are being honored.

Context continuity

Perhaps the most underdesigned element of modernization governance is the mechanism for maintaining context across organizational change. When a senior leader who has been deeply engaged in modernization governance transitions out of their role, the institutional knowledge they carry — about the architectural decisions that have been made, the reasoning behind them, the trade-offs that were evaluated and rejected, the commitments that were made to downstream stakeholders — typically walks out the door with them.

The organizational practices required to address this risk are straightforward but rarely implemented with sufficient discipline. Architectural decision records should be maintained in organizational repositories, not in individual files or email threads. Governance body membership transitions should include formal handover processes in which the incoming member is briefed on the institutional context required to participate effectively. And the modernization function should maintain a living narrative of the architectural journey — a document that describes where the organization has been, what it has learned, and where it is going —

that can orient new governance participants without requiring months of immersion to develop a working understanding.

Proportionality

The fifth component of effective governance is proportionality: calibrating the governance overhead to the significance of the decisions being made. Over-governed modernization — in which every architectural decision requires formal approval, every change goes through a heavyweight review process, and governance bodies are convened for decisions that could be made at lower levels of the organization — produces the bureaucratic friction that makes governance a synonym for slowness in many practitioners' experience.

Under-governed modernization — in which significant architectural decisions are made without adequate cross-functional perspective, investment commitments are made without accountability mechanisms, and execution proceeds without strategic oversight — produces the governance failures described earlier in this chapter.

Proportional governance calibrates the rigor of the governance process to the significance and reversibility of the decision. Decisions that are highly significant and difficult to reverse — major platform choices, significant investment commitments, architectural direction changes — warrant heavyweight governance processes. Decisions that are less significant or more easily reversible — implementation choices within an established architectural framework, resource allocation within approved budgets — should be made at the appropriate organizational level without requiring governance body involvement.

Building governance in practice

With the first-principles foundation established, this section works through the practical design of modernization governance structures. There is no single right design — the appropriate structure depends on organizational size, complexity, existing governance maturity, and cultural norms around decision-making. What follows is a framework for thinking through the design, with specific guidance on the most common organizational contexts.

The governance architecture

Effective modernization governance typically operates through three distinct but connected layers, each serving a different governance function at a different organizational level and time horizon.

The strategic governance layer is the executive-level body that owns the investment decisions, strategic direction, and accountability for modernization outcomes. In most organizations, this is a technology steering committee or an equivalent body that includes the CEO or COO, the CFO, the CTO, and senior representatives from the major business domains. This body typically meets quarterly and focuses on the questions that require cross-functional judgment at the most senior level: are we investing at the right level? Are our architectural choices aligned with our strategic direction? Are we making progress at the pace the organization requires?

The architectural governance layer is the technical body that maintains the integrity of architectural decisions across the distributed execution of modernization work. This is typically led by the principal architect or chief architect and includes the lead architects from each major business domain. This body typically meets monthly and focuses on the questions that require deep architectural judgment: are the choices being made by individual teams coherent with the overall architectural direction? Are there cross-cutting dependencies or conflicts that require resolution at the architectural level? Are the architectural standards and principles that guide execution still appropriate, or do they need to be updated in light of evolving circumstances?

The operational governance layer is the working-level body that manages the day-to-day execution of modernization work —

tracking progress, managing dependencies and conflicts between active workstreams, surfacing issues that require escalation to higher governance layers. This body typically meets weekly and includes the leads of the active modernization workstreams. Its job is operational coordination, not strategic direction — but it is the layer at which most governance failures first become visible, and a well-functioning operational governance layer is the earliest warning system for strategic and architectural governance issues.

Designing the strategic governance body

The strategic governance body is the most important governance structure in the modernization system, and the one most commonly designed inadequately. Two design choices are particularly consequential.

The first is membership composition. The strategic governance body must include the people who can make consequential decisions about modernization investment and direction — which means it must include the executives who control the relevant budgets, the executives who own the strategic priorities that modernization is meant to serve, and the technical leadership with the credibility to represent architectural reality accurately. Bodies that include the right titles but not the right people — where the actual decision-makers are represented by delegates who lack authority — are governance in form only.

The second is decision preparation. The quality of governance body decisions is a direct function of the quality of the information and analysis that members receive before they convene. Governance bodies that receive raw program status reports and are expected to derive strategic insight from them will not produce good strategic decisions. The modernization function must invest in preparing governance-quality briefings — documents that present the architectural situation, the investment trade-offs, and the decision options in terms that allow non-technical executives to engage substantively. This preparation takes time and skill, but it is among the highest-leverage investments the modernization function can make.

Designing the architectural governance body

The architectural governance body faces a different design challenge: maintaining sufficient rigor to catch the decisions that genuinely require cross-cutting architectural perspective, without becoming a bureaucratic bottleneck that slows execution.

The most effective architectural governance designs distinguish between decisions that require governance body review and decisions that can be made within established parameters without review. A well-designed architectural governance body reviews: choices of platforms or technologies outside the endorsed list; integration patterns that create new cross-domain dependencies; architectural decisions that affect multiple teams or domains; and any decision that would significantly constrain future architectural options. It does not review: implementation choices within established patterns; resource allocation within approved workstreams; or operational decisions that fall clearly within established parameters.

The architectural governance body should also invest explicitly in building shared architectural context across its members. The most valuable governance sessions are often not the formal reviews but the working sessions in which architects from different domains share what they are learning in their respective areas of the environment — surfacing emerging patterns, identifying potential cross-domain dependencies, and building the shared understanding of the environment that allows architectural decisions to be made consistently.

The governance calendar

One of the most practical and most neglected aspects of governance design is the governance calendar: an explicit schedule of when different governance bodies meet, what they review, and how information flows between governance layers.

Without a designed governance calendar, governance tends to happen reactively — in response to crises or at the convenience of the most senior participants — rather than proactively and consistently.

Governance layer	Meeting cadence	Primary agenda	Key inputs	Key outputs
Strategic	Quarterly	Investment priorities, architectural direction, outcome review	Architectural health report, strategic alignment assessment, investment performance	Investment decisions, direction adjustments, accountability consequences
Architectural	Monthly	Cross-domain coherence, standards review, emerging issues	Team architectural decisions, dependency analysis, standards compliance	Architectural guidance, standards updates, cross-domain coordination
Operational	Weekly	Execution progress, dependency management, issue resolution	Workstream status, risk register, escalations	Coordination decisions, risk escalations, governance briefings

Modernization governance calendar framework

The political reality of modernization governance

Governance design is organizational design, and organizational design is political. The most well-conceived governance structure will fail if it does not account for the political dynamics of the organization it is meant to operate within. This section addresses the political realities that modernization governance must navigate — not to be cynical about them, but to be realistic about the organizational work required to build and protect governance that can actually do its job.

Building the coalition

Effective modernization governance requires a coalition of senior leaders who understand the case for sustained architectural investment and are prepared to defend it when the competing pressures arise. Building this coalition is not primarily a technical communication challenge. It is a relationship-building challenge, and it takes time.

The most important relationships to build are with the senior leaders who control the budgets that modernization investment must compete for, and the senior leaders who most directly experience the operational and strategic consequences of architectural constraint. These two groups are not always the same, and their motivations for supporting modernization governance are often different. The CFO may be most persuaded by the cost argument — the maintenance burden that is consuming investment that could go to new capability development. The COO may be most persuaded by the operational risk argument — the incidents and delays that architectural fragility creates. The CEO may be most persuaded by the strategic optionality argument — the initiatives that cannot be pursued because the architecture will not support them.

Understanding the motivations of each coalition member, and framing the case for modernization governance in the terms most relevant to each, is one of the most important skills that modernization leaders need to develop. The architecture itself does not make the political case. The modernization leader does.

Surviving leadership transitions

Leadership transitions are the most significant threat to modernization governance continuity, and they are inevitable over any meaningful modernization timeline. The question is not whether they will occur but whether the governance structures are robust enough to survive them.

The most important protection against leadership transition disruption is the depth of institutional embedding of the governance structures themselves. Governance that is embodied in organizational roles and processes — that is described in organizational charters, built into regular governance calendars, and supported by documented architectural decision records — is more resilient than governance that exists primarily in the relationships and commitments of specific individuals.

When a leadership transition is anticipated, the modernization function should proactively invest in transition preparation: briefing incoming leaders on the architectural context, presenting the investment rationale in terms relevant to their priorities, and explicitly seeking their engagement in the governance structures rather than assuming their support. This is not about manipulation — it is about treating incoming leaders as the intelligent, consequential people they are and giving them the information they need to make good decisions.

When a transition results in governance disruption — when an incoming leader proposes changes that would undermine the architectural direction or investment level — the appropriate response is transparent engagement rather than institutional resistance. Present the case for continuity clearly, explain the consequences of the proposed changes in terms that connect to the incoming leader's priorities, and be genuinely open to direction changes that are strategically warranted. Not every inherited architectural commitment should be defended — some reflect outdated priorities. But the conversation should happen explicitly and with full information, not by default or through organizational attrition.

Protecting modernization investment through budget cycles

Annual budget cycles are a recurring threat to modernization governance continuity. The dynamics are predictable: modernization investment is large and ongoing; its returns are deferred and diffuse; and at every budget cycle, there will be competing priorities with more immediate and visible returns competing for the same resources. Without governance mechanisms specifically designed to protect modernization investment, budget cycles will systematically erode it.

Several mechanisms can strengthen investment protection. The first is explicit multi-year investment commitments: governance decisions that commit to modernization investment levels over a defined multi-year horizon, requiring a formal governance decision to revisit rather than allowing the investment level to be renegotiated at each annual cycle. These commitments are not irrevocable — circumstances change and investment levels should be able to respond — but they create a presumption of continuity that places the burden of justification on reduction rather than on continuation.

The second is outcome-linked investment: connecting modernization investment levels explicitly to the architectural health indicators and outcome metrics that the governance body tracks. When the governance body can see, in each budget cycle, the trajectory of technical debt, change velocity, and disruption rate alongside the investment that has been producing those outcomes, the investment decision is grounded in evidence rather than competing primarily on the basis of organizational priority.

The third is risk-explicit investment decisions: making the cost of not investing — the expected operational risk, the foregone strategic options, the compounding maintenance burden — explicit in the budget cycle conversation. Investment decisions made without full visibility of the cost of the alternative are systematically biased toward underinvestment. Making the risk explicit corrects this bias.

Managing the tension between governance and execution speed

The most common complaint about modernization governance from practitioners is that it slows things down. This complaint is sometimes valid and sometimes not, and distinguishing between the two is important.

When governance is slowing things down because it is exercising appropriate scrutiny over significant decisions, the slowdown is the governance doing its job. A major platform choice that takes an extra two weeks to clear architectural governance because the implications for cross-domain dependencies were not initially visible is a governance success — the two weeks invested up front prevented months of rework that would have followed an unconsidered decision.

When governance is slowing things down because the governance process is requiring approval for decisions that fall clearly within established parameters, because governance bodies are not meeting frequently enough to maintain decision momentum, or because the information preparation required for governance participation is consuming more time than the decisions warrant, the slowdown is a governance design failure. Fixing it requires governance redesign — clearer decision authority, more frequent operational governance, better information infrastructure — not a reduction in governance rigor.

The modernization function has a responsibility to distinguish between these cases and to advocate for governance redesign when the governance process is genuinely impeding execution rather than appropriately scrutinizing it. This requires the organizational credibility and the relationship with governance leadership that allows this kind of direct feedback to be heard constructively.

TOOL — MODERNIZATION GOVERNANCE DESIGN WORKSHEET

Use this worksheet when designing or redesigning modernization governance structures. Work through each section in sequence.

Decision inventory: List the ten most consequential decisions your modernization program will need to make over the next two years. For each, identify: which organizational level should own this decision, what information is required to make it well, and who needs to be involved for the decision to be organizationally legitimate.

Governance body design: For each governance layer (strategic, architectural, operational), define: who are the members, what authority do they have, how often do they meet, what decisions do they make vs. review vs. advise on, and what information do they receive.

Information architecture: Map how information flows from execution to governance. Who produces the architectural health report? Who translates technical complexity into governance-quality briefings? What is the preparation cadence and the format for each governance layer?

Commitment mechanisms: How will governance decisions be recorded and made durable? Where are architectural decision records maintained? What is the process for revisiting a committed architectural direction? What budget mechanisms protect modernization investment between cycles?

Continuity design: What happens when a key governance participant transitions out of their role? Who maintains the institutional context? What is the handover process? Where is the organizational narrative maintained?

Coalition map: Who are the five or six senior leaders whose sustained engagement is most important to governance effectiveness? What motivates each of them to support modernization investment? What is the current state of your relationship with each, and what would strengthen it?

TOOL — GOVERNANCE HEALTH CHECK (EXPANDED)

Use this health check annually to assess the quality of your modernization governance and identify the most important areas for improvement.

Decision quality: When you look back at significant modernization decisions made in the past year, were they made with adequate information, at the right organizational level, with genuine cross-functional input? Or were they made too quickly, with inadequate information, or without the perspectives required to make them well?

Information quality: Do governance body members receive information that genuinely informs their decisions, or do they receive status reports that tell them what has been done without giving them the context to evaluate whether it is the right thing to be doing?

Commitment durability: Look at the architectural commitments made two or three years ago. Are they still intact? If not, were they changed through deliberate governance decisions with full information, or were they quietly eroded through budget reallocation, leadership inattention, or organizational drift?

Leadership depth: If your two most engaged senior governance participants left their roles tomorrow, would the governance structures survive? Or would governance effectiveness collapse to the baseline of whoever replaced them?

Execution relationship: Do the practitioners doing modernization execution feel that governance is an asset to their work — that it provides the strategic direction, the investment protection, and the organizational authority that helps them do their jobs? Or do they feel that governance is primarily an obstacle?

Political resilience: When budget pressure has arisen in the past year, how well did modernization investment hold? Was it protected by governance mechanisms, defended by committed leaders, or did it erode? What does this tell you about the strength of the governance coalition?

CHAPTER 10

Making Modernization Continuous

How to transition from episodic transformation programs to a permanent organizational function — the staffing models, funding structures, transition process, and institutional habits that sustain continuous architectural evolution

---

Everything in this book leads here. The framework, the dimensions, the tools — they are only valuable if the organization has the structural foundation to apply them continuously, over time, as a normal dimension of institutional management rather than as a periodic special effort. That structural foundation is what this chapter is about.

The transition from episodic modernization to continuous evolution is the hardest organizational change in the Modernization Intelligence journey. It requires changes in how the work is conceptualized, organized, funded, and measured. It requires building new institutional habits and retiring old ones. And it requires sustaining the organizational will to make these changes through a period when the returns on the investment are not yet fully visible.

This chapter works through the transition in full: what it means to move from a program to a function, how that transition actually happens in practice, what the right staffing model looks like and how to build it, how to make the case for operational funding and how to manage the transition from capital to operational budget models, what day-to-day continuous evolution looks like in organizations that have achieved it, and how to build and sustain the institutional habits that are the long-term foundation of the capability.

From program to function: understanding the transition

The distinction between a program and a function is more than organizational vocabulary. It reflects a fundamentally different theory of what the work is and how it should be organized.

A program is organized around a deliverable. It exists to produce a defined outcome — a migrated system, a replaced platform, a modernized architecture — and once that outcome has been produced, the program's reason for existing is gone. Programs are the right organizational unit for work that genuinely has an endpoint. They are the wrong organizational unit for work that does not.

A function is organized around a capability. It exists to maintain and develop the organization's ability to do something — not to produce a one-time outcome but to deliver ongoing value. Finance functions do not exist to produce a specific set of financial statements; they exist to maintain the organization's capacity to manage its finances accurately and responsibly, indefinitely. HR functions do not exist to complete a hiring cycle; they exist to maintain the organization's capacity to attract, develop, and retain the talent it needs, continuously.

A modernization function exists to maintain the organization's capacity to evolve its software environment — to keep its architecture aligned with its operational and strategic needs, continuously, as those needs change over time. This is not a finite deliverable. It is an ongoing organizational responsibility, and the function that carries it should be organized accordingly.

The organizational symptoms of program thinking

Before describing how to make the transition, it is worth recognizing the organizational symptoms that indicate program thinking is still operating. These symptoms are common, and recognizing them is the first step toward addressing them.

Modernization investment is justified through project business cases. Each round of investment requires a new business case with a defined ROI horizon, rather than being treated as an ongoing operational investment whose justification is the sustained architectural quality it maintains.

The modernization team reassembles at the beginning of each program. The people doing modernization work are brought together from other roles or hired externally when a program begins, and dispersed back to their previous roles or let go when it concludes. There is no stable institutional knowledge that accumulates across program cycles.

Completion is celebrated as an endpoint. When a program delivers its defined scope, the organization communicates it as a completion — in leadership communications, in board reporting, in organizational narratives. The implicit message is that the work is done. And then, some years later, it begins again.

Technical debt is managed reactively. Technical debt accumulates between programs because there is no ongoing investment in retiring it. It is addressed in large batches, during programs, after it has grown to the point where it is impairing operations. The gradual, continuous work of keeping debt from accumulating in the first place is not organized or funded.

What the transition requires

Transitioning from program to function requires changes across five organizational dimensions. Each dimension is interconnected — partial transitions that address some dimensions but not others tend to revert, because the unchanged dimensions pull the organization back toward its previous mode of operation.

Mandate: the modernization function needs an explicit, board-level-endorsed mandate that defines its ongoing responsibility for architectural quality as an institutional priority. Without this mandate, the function's authority is contingent on the support of current leadership rather than embedded in institutional structure.

Leadership: the modernization function needs a permanent leadership role — a chief modernization officer, a VP of Modernization, a chief architect with explicit modernization accountability — that is a regular member of the institutional leadership team. This is not a program director role that exists for the duration of a specific initiative. It is a permanent institutional role with ongoing accountability.

Team: the function needs a permanent core team with stable membership, not a project team that assembles and disperses. The institutional knowledge that accumulates in a stable team over years of continuous modernization work is one of the most valuable assets the function builds, and it is lost every time the team disbands.

Budget: the function needs an operational budget that persists across planning cycles, not a capital appropriation for specific programs. This is the change that most directly signals the organizational intent to treat modernization as a permanent function.

Metrics: the function needs to be evaluated on indicators of ongoing architectural improvement — technical debt trajectory, change velocity, strategic capability enablement — not on program delivery metrics. Evaluation frameworks shape organizational behavior, and evaluation frameworks that reward program completion will produce program thinking even within a nominally permanent function.

How the transition actually happens

Describing the desired end state of the transition is easier than describing how to get there. Most organizations cannot simply declare that they are transitioning from programs to a function and have it be so. The transition takes place in the context of existing organizational structures, existing funding models, existing leadership expectations, and existing cultural norms that resist change. A realistic transition plan must work within these constraints.

Phase one: building the case

The transition begins with the case-making work described in Chapter Three — establishing a credible estimate of the cost of the current approach and the value of the alternative. This case needs to be made to the specific decision-makers who have the authority to authorize the structural changes that the transition requires: the CFO who will need to approve the reclassification of modernization investment from capital to operational budget, the CEO who will need to endorse the creation of a permanent leadership role, and the board members who will need to understand why this is a strategic investment rather than a technology overhead.

The case should be grounded in specific institutional experience: the programs that have not produced durable improvement, the architectural constraints that have limited strategic options, the costs that have been incurred as a result. Abstract arguments about the value of continuous modernization are less persuasive than concrete analysis of what the current approach has cost and what a different approach would enable.

Phase two: piloting the function model

Rather than attempting to transition the entire modernization effort from program to function in a single step, most organizations benefit from piloting the function model in a bounded domain before attempting the full transition. Choose a domain — a specific business area, a specific application portfolio, a specific technology layer — and organize modernization in that domain as a permanent function: stable team, operational budget, outcome metrics, governance integration.

The pilot serves two purposes. First, it produces evidence of what the function model can deliver — evidence that is far more persuasive than any argument in the abstract. When the governance body can see, in a specific domain, that a stable modernization team with operational funding is producing better architectural outcomes at lower cost than the program model produced in comparable domains, the case for broader transition is made by experience rather than by argument.

Second, the pilot builds the organizational capability required for the full transition. The staffing model, the funding structures, the governance integration, the measurement approach — all of these need to be worked out in practice, and the pilot is the place to work them out at manageable scale before attempting them organization-wide.

Phase three: scaling the transition

Once the pilot has established proof of concept and built organizational confidence in the function model, the transition can be extended to additional domains. This extension should be managed sequentially rather than simultaneously — adding domains to the function model one or two at a time, with each addition benefiting from the learning of the previous ones.

The most important aspect of scaling the transition is maintaining the organizational attention required to do each extension well. Transitions that are rushed — that attempt to move too many domains into the function model simultaneously before the model is mature — tend to produce partial transitions that have the form of a function but the substance of a program.

Building and staffing the modernization function

The staffing question for a permanent modernization function is different from the staffing question for a program, and it deserves more specific treatment than it typically receives.

The core team structure

The core modernization function team needs three distinct capability clusters, and the team structure should be designed to ensure all three are present and integrated.

Architectural intelligence is the capability to understand the environment deeply and maintain that understanding over time. People in this capability cluster are responsible for architectural awareness: running the systems inventory, maintaining the dependency map, keeping the knowledge base current, and synthesizing what they know into the architectural context that drives sequencing and governance decisions. This work requires deep technical knowledge of the environment — not generic architecture skill but specific, accumulated knowledge of the institution's actual systems. It is the capability that is hardest to hire from outside and most valuable to develop internally.

Transformation strategy is the capability to translate architectural knowledge into effective transformation plans and to update those plans as circumstances change. People in this capability cluster are responsible for sequencing and roadmapping: analyzing the dependency landscape, building and maintaining the transformation roadmap, evaluating the risk-value trade-offs of competing sequencing options, and translating strategic priorities into architectural actions. This work combines technical judgment with strategic thinking in a way that is genuinely rare — the people who can do it well are among the most valuable members of the modernization function.

Execution leadership is the capability to lead and manage the execution of transformation work: assembling and directing the execution teams, managing the dependencies and risks that emerge during implementation, maintaining execution discipline across extended delivery timelines, and building the organizational relationships that make complex change possible. This is a program management capability at its core, but one that requires enough technical grounding to engage credibly with the architectural and engineering decisions that arise during execution.

The talent profile

The talent profile for the modernization function is genuinely unusual, and it is worth being explicit about what to look for when building or evaluating the team.

Technical depth without technical narrowness. The people in the core team need to understand the technology environment deeply — at the level of actual systems and actual code, not just architectural abstractions. But they also need to be able to operate across the full breadth of the environment, which in a mature institutional context means navigating multiple technology generations, multiple platform paradigms, and multiple technical domains. The technically narrow specialist who knows one system or one technology well but cannot engage with the broader environment is not the right profile.

Strategic judgment alongside technical knowledge. The modernization function needs people who can connect architectural decisions to institutional strategy — who understand not just what the technology should do but why it matters, and who can translate that connection into terms that resonate with non-technical leaders. This strategic orientation is not common among technically deep individuals, and finding it requires being explicit about it in hiring conversations.

Organizational effectiveness. Modernization requires navigating complex organizational terrain: building the relationships that make change possible, managing the competing interests of different organizational constituencies, communicating complex trade-offs in accessible terms, and sustaining organizational momentum through the extended timelines and competing pressures that modernization involves. Technical and strategic capability without organizational effectiveness is common; the full combination is rare and should be weighted heavily in hiring decisions.

Learning orientation. Perhaps the most important long-term quality in modernization function members is the genuine orientation toward learning: the intellectual curiosity and the professional discipline to extract lessons from experience, to update their understanding when evidence contradicts their expectations, and to apply what they have learned to subsequent decisions. The modernization function is the organizational mechanism through which the institution learns from its architectural experience. People who do not learn from their own experience cannot build or sustain that mechanism.

Building from what you have

Few organizations building a modernization function for the first time will be starting with a team that has all of the capabilities described above. The more common starting point is a handful of technically strong individuals who have been doing modernization work within the program model — people who have deep knowledge of the environment but who have been organized around specific programs rather than as a continuous function.

Building from this starting point requires being honest about the gaps and deliberate about how to close them. The gaps are usually in strategic judgment and organizational effectiveness rather than in technical knowledge. Addressing them requires both hiring decisions — bringing in people who have demonstrated these capabilities in other contexts — and development investments for existing team members: exposure to strategic planning processes, relationships with senior leaders, and the experience of operating in governance conversations rather than purely in technical ones.

The funding transition: from capital to operational

The funding model transition is the organizational change that most directly signals the intent to treat modernization as a permanent function, and it is often the hardest to achieve. Understanding the specific arguments that make the transition possible — and the specific objections that must be addressed — is essential for modernization leaders making this case.

Why capital funding produces program behavior

Capital funding is designed for investments with defined scopes, defined timelines, and defined returns. When a project is capitalized, it is because the investment is expected to produce a specific, bounded asset — a building, a system, a piece of equipment — whose value can be defined and depreciated over time. The governance structures around capital investment are designed to evaluate these bounded investments: is the defined scope appropriate? Is the return on the defined investment adequate? Is the timeline realistic?

Modernization work does not fit this structure. The architectural quality that sustained modernization investment maintains is not a bounded asset that can be defined and depreciated. It is an ongoing organizational condition — the health of the environment — that requires continuous investment to maintain. Capitalized modernization investment produces the same governance structures as any other capital project: defined scope, defined timeline, defined completion criterion. And those governance structures produce program behavior, regardless of the organization's stated intent.

Making the case for operational funding

The argument for operational funding is straightforward once the analogy to other organizational functions is made clearly. Organizations do not capitalize their finance function because they expect it to eventually complete its work and be shut down. They fund it operationally because it is a permanent organizational function that requires ongoing investment to maintain. The same logic applies to the modernization function.

The CFO objection most commonly encountered is that operational budget is subject to more rigorous ongoing scrutiny than capital budget — that operational spending must justify itself in each budget cycle rather than being committed over a multi-year capital program. This objection is actually an argument for operational funding from the modernization function's perspective: a modernization function that is producing measurable architectural improvement should be able to justify its investment in every budget cycle, and the outcome metrics described in this chapter provide the basis for doing so.

The deeper CFO concern is typically that operational funding creates an ongoing cost that does not feel like it is earning its return. Addressing this concern requires connecting the operational budget explicitly to the cost savings it is producing: the maintenance cost reduction, the rework cost reduction, the manual compensation cost reduction that ongoing modernization investment is generating. When the modernization function can demonstrate, in each budget cycle, that its operational investment is producing cost savings that exceed its cost, the case for continued operational funding is made by evidence.

Managing the transition period

The transition from capital to operational funding rarely happens in a single budget cycle. Most organizations go through a transition period in which modernization investment is partially capitalized and partially operational — with the balance shifting toward operational as the function model matures and the evidence base for its value accumulates.

During this transition period, the most important financial management task is maintaining clear accounting of what is being funded as capital versus operational, and ensuring that the operational component is treated as a genuine permanent commitment rather than as a capital project with a different label. The transition period should have a defined endpoint — a specific year by which the full modernization function investment will be operational — rather than remaining permanently in a hybrid state.

What continuous evolution looks like day to day

One of the most useful things this chapter can offer is a concrete description of what continuous evolution looks like in organizations that have achieved it — what the modernization function does on a daily, weekly, monthly, and quarterly basis. This description is necessarily a generalization; the specifics vary by organizational size and context. But the shape of the work is recognizable across contexts.

Daily

Daily work in a mature modernization function is primarily execution work: the active management of transformation initiatives currently in progress. Execution leads are monitoring the observability dashboards for the systems being changed, reviewing test results from ongoing development work, managing the dependencies between active workstreams, and addressing the operational questions and issues that arise in the course of any complex change program.

Daily work also includes the ongoing maintenance of architectural awareness: updating the dependency map when new integrations are created, documenting the behavioral patterns observed during execution work, and capturing the architectural knowledge surfaced by operational incidents. This is unglamorous work. It is also the work that prevents the architectural knowledge base from decaying and that ensures the information foundation for subsequent modernization decisions remains accurate.

Weekly

Weekly work centers on the operational governance layer: the cross-team coordination meeting at which active workstream leads share progress, surface dependencies and conflicts, and raise issues that require escalation or cross-team resolution. This meeting is the heartbeat of the modernization function — the regular rhythm that maintains organizational cohesion across the distributed execution of modernization work.

Weekly work also includes the ongoing sequencing analysis: reviewing the transformation roadmap in light of execution progress and emerging information, identifying any adjustments required to the planned sequence, and preparing the input to the next architectural governance session.

Monthly

Monthly work centers on the architectural governance layer: the cross-domain architect meeting at which the coherence of architectural decisions across active workstreams is reviewed, emerging cross-cutting dependencies are identified and addressed, and the architectural standards and principles are assessed for continued appropriateness.

Monthly work also includes the preparation of governance-quality reporting for the strategic governance body: the architectural health update that translates the current state of the environment, the progress of active transformation work, and the trajectory of the key outcome metrics into the terms that executive governance participants need to exercise meaningful oversight.

Quarterly

Quarterly work centers on the strategic governance layer: the executive governance meeting at which investment priorities are reviewed, strategic alignment is assessed, and significant decisions about modernization direction and investment level are made. Preparing for this meeting — building the briefing materials, preparing the investment case for any decisions required, pre-briefing key participants — is a significant periodic investment for the modernization function leadership.

Quarterly work also includes the formal retrospective: the structured, cross-team examination of what the modernization function has learned in the past quarter and how that learning should affect the work going forward. The retrospective is described in more detail in the institutional habits section below.

Building and sustaining institutional habits

The organizational structures, funding models, and staffing designs described in this chapter are necessary but not sufficient for continuous evolution. What makes the capability durable — what prevents it from degrading back toward the program model when organizational pressures arise — is a set of institutional habits: recurring practices and cultural norms that make architectural improvement a normal, expected dimension of how the organization operates.

Habits are different from processes. A process is a defined sequence of steps that is followed because it is required. A habit is a practice that is followed because it has become natural — because the organization would feel that something was missing if it did not happen, rather than feeling that a requirement was being met when it did. Building genuine institutional habits takes years. But the investment is worth making, because habits are far more resilient than processes under organizational pressure.

The retrospective habit

The retrospective is the most important institutional habit in a continuous evolution capability. A well-run modernization retrospective is not a status meeting, and it is not a post-mortem. It is a structured organizational learning session: a deliberate examination of what has been done, what it produced, what was learned, and what should be done differently as a result.

The questions that a useful modernization retrospective asks are specific. What modernization work was completed in the past quarter? What was the expected impact of that work, and what was the actual impact? Where did the execution differ from the plan, and what does that difference tell us about our understanding of the environment? What did we learn about the dependency landscape that we did not know before? What did we learn about our execution capability — where were we more effective than expected, and where did we struggle? What should we do differently in the next quarter as a result?

The retrospective output is not just a learning document — it is an update to the organizational knowledge base. The dependency mappings that were revealed by execution experience should be added to the architectural knowledge base. The sequencing decisions that turned out to be suboptimal should be analyzed and their lessons captured. The execution practices that worked better or worse than expected should be noted and communicated to the broader execution community.

Making the retrospective a genuine institutional habit requires protecting it. When execution pressure is high — when there is a critical delivery in progress, when the organization is in the middle of a significant challenge — the retrospective is the first thing that gets cancelled. The organizational discipline required is to protect the retrospective even under pressure, because the times of highest execution intensity are precisely the times when the most learning is available to be captured.

The architectural debt recognition habit

Technical debt is most manageable when it is recognized and documented at the moment of creation, not when it has grown large enough to cause operational problems. Building the habit of immediate debt recognition requires a cultural norm: when a pragmatic shortcut is taken — a quick integration that bypasses the established integration platform, a configuration change that creates an undocumented behavioral dependency, a design decision that defers complexity rather than addressing it — that shortcut is documented immediately, sized approximately, and added to the architectural debt register.

This habit is culturally counter-intuitive in many organizations. Engineers and architects are often reluctant to document debt they have created, for the same reasons that people are reluctant to document their own mistakes: it feels like an admission of inadequacy. Building the cultural reframe required to make debt recognition a normal, expected practice — framing it as professional discipline rather than personal accountability, and connecting it to the organizational outcome of maintaining accurate architectural knowledge — takes deliberate leadership attention.

The practical mechanism that makes debt recognition sustainable is integration with the existing development workflow. When debt recognition is a separate, additional activity that requires a separate effort to perform, it will not be performed consistently under execution pressure. When it is a standard element of the development process — a required field in the change management system, a standing agenda item in the weekly engineering review — it becomes part of the normal rhythm rather than an additional burden.

The continuous discovery habit

Architectural debt and complexity accumulate fastest in the parts of the environment that are not receiving active attention. The systems that have not been touched in years, the integrations that were built as temporary solutions and never revisited, the organizational dependencies that were established a decade ago and have never been examined — these are the places where the surprises that derail modernization programs are most likely to be hiding.

The continuous discovery habit is the practice of regularly examining the less-attended parts of the environment: a periodic, structured survey of systems and integrations that have not been the focus of recent modernization work, specifically looking for the accumulation of complexity and debt that occurs in low-visibility areas. This is not the same as the comprehensive systems inventory described in Chapter Six — it is lighter, more targeted, and specifically focused on the areas most likely to have changed without being noticed.

A practical approach to continuous discovery is to assign rotating responsibility for it to members of the modernization function: each quarter, a different team member takes on the responsibility of examining a specific area of the environment that has not been recently reviewed, producing a brief assessment of what they find and whether it warrants more structured attention. This keeps the discovery habit alive without requiring a dedicated discovery team.

The knowledge transfer habit

The institutional knowledge of the modernization function — the accumulated understanding of the environment, the lessons from years of transformation work, the architectural reasoning that informs current decisions — is among the function's most valuable assets and among its most fragile. It is fragile because it is tacit: it lives in the heads of the people who have accumulated it, and it is at risk every time one of those people leaves the organization.

The knowledge transfer habit is the practice of continuously converting tacit knowledge into explicit organizational knowledge: the architectural decision records that document not just what was decided but why, the lessons-learned documents that capture what was learned from specific transformation experiences, the onboarding processes that systematically transfer institutional context to new team members, and the regular knowledge-sharing sessions at which experienced team members share their understanding of specific parts of the environment with colleagues who have not worked in those areas.

This habit requires the organizational recognition that knowledge transfer is a legitimate use of modernization function time — that it is not overhead, not a distraction from the real work, but an essential investment in the durability of the capability itself. Building this recognition into the evaluation and incentive structures of the function is important: if knowledge transfer is valued only in rhetoric but not in practice, the competing pressures of execution will consistently crowd it out.

The learning culture

Underlying all of the specific habits described above is a more fundamental cultural characteristic: a genuine organizational orientation toward learning. Organizations with a learning culture treat mistakes as information rather than as accountability events, update their understanding when evidence contradicts their expectations, and create the psychological safety required for honest retrospectives and open knowledge sharing.

Building a learning culture in the modernization function requires deliberate leadership action. Leaders who treat execution failures as occasions for blame rather than for understanding will produce teams that hide problems rather than surface them. Leaders who treat architectural surprises as evidence of team incompetence rather than as evidence of architectural complexity will produce teams that underreport what they are discovering. Leaders who treat their own certainty as a virtue rather than as a risk will produce teams that stop challenging assumptions.

The counterpart to this is leaders who model the learning behaviors they want to see: who acknowledge what they got wrong in retrospectives, who update their architectural views when new information arrives, who treat the team's collective knowledge as more reliable than any individual's judgment, and who create the conditions in which honest, uncomfortable information can surface safely.

Continuous evolution is not a capability that organizations build and then have. It is a capability that organizations continuously build — through the accumulated investment of consistent attention, honest learning, and the institutional discipline to maintain that attention through the competing pressures that will always be present.

TOOL — CONTINUOUS EVOLUTION READINESS ASSESSMENT (EXPANDED)

This assessment evaluates your organization's readiness across all dimensions of the continuous evolution transition. Use it to identify the most important gaps and the highest-leverage investments for your specific situation.

Organizational structure: Does modernization have a permanent organizational home with a mandate, named leadership, and ongoing accountabilities? Is that structure described in organizational documents rather than existing only in informal understanding? Score 1 if modernization is organized as a series of programs; 5 if there is a named, permanent modernization function with board-level recognition.

Funding model: Is the modernization function funded through an operational budget that persists across planning cycles? Has the organization made a formal commitment to treat modernization investment as operational rather than capital? Score 1 if all modernization investment is capitalized as specific programs; 5 if the full core function is operationally funded with multi-year commitment.

Staffing continuity: Does the modernization function have a stable core team with at least two or three years of accumulated institutional knowledge? Is there an explicit knowledge transfer practice that protects institutional knowledge from attrition? Score 1 if the team assembles fresh for each program; 5 if there is a stable core team with documented knowledge transfer practices.

Retrospective practice: Does the modernization function conduct formal retrospectives on a regular cadence — at least quarterly — that produce documented learning and visible changes to subsequent work? Score 1 if retrospectives are ad hoc or absent; 5 if they are protected, structured, well-attended, and demonstrably influence subsequent decisions.

Debt recognition: Is architectural debt recognized and documented at the moment of creation, through practices integrated into the development workflow? Does the architectural debt register reflect current reality or only the debt that has become large enough to cause problems? Score 1 if debt is discovered reactively; 5 if there is a functioning debt recognition practice with a current, maintained register.

Continuous discovery: Is there a regular practice of examining the less-attended parts of the environment for accumulating complexity and debt? Score 1 if discovery only happens at the start of programs; 5 if there is a regular, distributed discovery practice that keeps the architectural knowledge base current across the full environment.

Learning culture: Does the modernization function's culture support honest retrospectives, open surfacing of problems, and updating of views when evidence warrants it? Do leaders model the learning behaviors they want to see? Score 1 if failures are treated primarily as accountability events; 5 if there is a genuine learning culture with psychological safety and leader-modeled learning behaviors.

Scoring: 28-35 — mature continuous evolution capability. 20-27 — developing capability with meaningful gaps; prioritize the lowest-scoring dimensions. 12-19 — early stage; focus on organizational structure, funding model, and staffing continuity as the foundational changes that enable everything else. Below 12 — program thinking is still dominant; the transition roadmap in this chapter should be the near-term priority.

Chapters Nine and Ten together describe the organizational foundation on which Modernization Intelligence rests. Governance alignment ensures that the capability is connected to institutional strategy, protected from the organizational pressures that would otherwise erode it, and accountable for the outcomes it is designed to produce. Continuous evolution ensures that the capability is permanent — that the organization does not revert to the episodic program model the first time a competing priority appears.

Neither is easy. Both are essential. And both become easier as the capability matures: governance structures that have survived a leadership transition are more robust than ones that have not. A retrospective practice that has produced visible, consequential learning is more likely to be protected than one that is still establishing its value. The investment in building these foundations pays dividends that compound over time — which is the defining characteristic of the Modernization Intelligence discipline as a whole.

PART THREE

Putting It Into Practice

Four chapters that translate the framework into organizational action: assessing where you are, recognizing your situation, integrating AI tools effectively, and building the modernization function that makes everything else possible.

CHAPTER 11

Assessing Your Current Maturity

How to use the Modernization Maturity Curve as a working diagnostic — scoring your organization, interpreting the results, and building a roadmap from wherever you are

A framework is only useful if it can be applied. The Modernization Intelligence framework introduced in Part Two describes what mature organizational capability looks like across five dimensions. But knowing what mature looks like is not the same as knowing where your organization currently stands, what the most important gaps are, and what sequence of investments will move you most effectively toward the capability you need.

This chapter provides the diagnostic tools to answer those questions. It introduces a structured maturity assessment — a scoring instrument that produces a concrete picture of where your organization currently stands on each of the five dimensions of Modernization Intelligence, and across the three stages of the Modernization Maturity Curve. It then provides guidance on interpreting the results: understanding what the scores mean, identifying the highest-leverage investments, and building a realistic roadmap from your current position.

The assessment is designed to be completed by the modernization leadership team working together, not by a single individual. The most valuable part of the process is often the conversation that the scoring generates — the points of disagreement, the gaps between how different parts of the organization perceive their capability, and the specific evidence that supports or challenges any given score. Plan for two to three hours for a first-time assessment.

The Modernization Maturity Curve: a recap

The Modernization Maturity Curve describes three observable stages in the development of Modernization Intelligence. They are not prescriptive stages through which every organization must pass in sequence — some organizations will find that they have elements of multiple stages operating simultaneously in different parts of the organization. They are diagnostic stages: observable patterns that describe recognizable organizational conditions and that point toward the investments most likely to advance capability.

Reactive organizations treat modernization as a crisis response. Transformation work is initiated when architectural constraint becomes acute enough to threaten operations, compliance, or strategic execution. There is no sustained investment in architectural awareness, no structured sequencing capability, and no governance that can maintain coherence across multi-year timelines. Each program starts largely from scratch. The cost of modernization at this stage is high relative to the outcomes produced, because the absence of accumulated institutional knowledge means that every program pays the full price of discovery.

Structured organizations have developed the capability to plan and execute modernization programs with reasonable reliability. Governance structures exist for major initiatives. Some degree of architectural documentation is maintained. Technical teams have relevant expertise. Program success rates are meaningfully better than at the reactive stage. The limitation is that the program model still dominates: modernization is organized around bounded initiatives, architectural knowledge is allowed to decay between programs, and the compounding returns of continuous evolution are not being realized.

Institutionalized organizations treat modernization as a permanent organizational function. Architectural awareness is continuously maintained. Transformation sequencing is a regular strategic activity. Execution capability is embedded in organizational culture and practice. Governance structures maintain coherence across multi-year timelines. And the learning mechanisms of the continuous evolution discipline are generating compounding returns — each cycle of work building the capability for the next. At this stage, modernization is no longer experienced as a strategic initiative. It is simply how the organization manages its technological environment.

The Modernization Intelligence Maturity Assessment

The assessment that follows scores your organization across the five dimensions of Modernization Intelligence and then combines those dimension scores into an overall maturity profile. Each dimension is assessed across five indicators. Rate each indicator on a scale of one to four, where one means the capability described is absent or very early stage, two means it exists in partial form or inconsistently, three means it is present and functioning but not yet mature, and four means it is mature, consistently practiced, and producing measurable value.

Dimension 1 — Architectural Awareness

Indicator	1 — Absent	2 — Partial	3 — Functional	4 — Mature
Systems inventory	No current inventory of production systems; significant shadow IT undocumented	Formal systems registered; significant shadow IT not captured	Current inventory including most shadow IT; updated periodically	Comprehensive, continuously maintained inventory including all operational tools; integrated with change management

Dependency mapping	No documented dependencies; discovered when they break	Major integrations documented; implicit dependencies largely unknown	Core dependencies mapped; behavioral dependencies partially documented	Full dependency map maintained continuously; behavioral and organizational dependencies captured
Behavioral knowledge	System behavior known only by individuals; no documentation	Some behavioral documentation; significant tacit knowledge in individuals	Key system behaviors documented; knowledge transfer practices in place	Comprehensive behavioral documentation; tacit knowledge systematically captured; onboarding process transfers context
Currency mechanisms	No process for updating architectural knowledge	Ad hoc updates when major changes occur	Change-triggered updates in place; periodic verification conducted	Automated discovery integrated with change management; incident-driven learning practice active; quarterly verification
Decision utility	Architectural knowledge not used in	Occasionally referenced in planning; not	Regularly used in sequencing and	Primary input to all modernization decisions;

	modernization planning	systematically integrated	governance decisions	governance body explicitly requests and uses architectural intelligence

Dimension 2 — Transformation Sequencing

Indicator	1 — Absent	2 — Partial	3 — Functional	4 — Mature
Dependency analysis	No dependency analysis performed before transformation decisions	High-level dependency review; significant gaps	Structured dependency matrix built for major initiatives	Comprehensive dependency analysis; behavioral and organizational dependencies included; regularly updated
Risk calibration	Risk not explicitly assessed; sequence driven by business priority or convenience	High-level risk categorization; not systematically used in sequencing	Risk-value matrix used to inform sequencing decisions	Multi-dimensional risk assessment; explicit risk mitigation sequenced into roadmap; regularly reviewed

Roadmap quality	No transformation roadmap; work sequenced ad hoc	High-level roadmap exists; dependency ordering not explicit	Dependency-ordered roadmap maintained; preparation activities included	Living roadmap with documented sequencing rationale; regularly updated from execution learning; governance-reviewed
Sequencing continuity	Sequence reset with each new program	Roadmap persists within a program; not maintained across programs	Sequencing updated periodically; some continuity across program cycles	Continuous sequencing function; roadmap maintained and updated regardless of program boundaries
Strategic alignment	Transformation sequence driven by technical preference; no strategic connection	Business priority influences sequence; strategic connection not explicit	Transformation sequence explicitly connected to strategic priorities	Sequencing decisions documented with strategic rationale; governance body reviews alignment quarterly

Dimension 3 — Execution Discipline

Indicator	1 — Absent	2 — Partial	3 — Functional	4 — Mature

Incremental delivery	Large-batch changes; big-bang cutovers; limited production validation before full commitment	Some incremental elements; significant big-batch delivery still common	Incremental delivery practiced for most changes; feature toggles used	Consistently incremental; dark launches routine; production validation standard before full commitment
Observability	Limited visibility into system behavior during changes; problems discovered reactively	Basic monitoring in place; gaps in coverage for systems being changed	Observability established for most modernization work before changes begin	Comprehensive observability infrastructure; pre-change baseline captured; real-time behavior monitoring during all changes
Rollback capability	No rollback planning; rollback improvised if needed	Rollback considered; not always documented or tested	Rollback plans documented and reviewed before changes	Rollback plans documented, tested in staging, with explicit trigger conditions; data state management validated
Parallel operation	Single cutover; no parallel operation during migrations	Parallel operation used occasionally for high-risk changes	Parallel operation standard practice for significant migrations	Parallel operation with systematic output comparison; explicit cutover criteria; active

				validation during parallel period
Execution readiness	No formal readiness assessment; go/no-go decisions informal	Checklist-based readiness review; not consistently applied	Formal execution readiness assessment before all significant changes	Comprehensive readiness assessment across technical, operational, governance, and rollback dimensions; governance sign-off required

Dimension 4 — Governance Alignment

Indicator	1 — Absent	2 — Partial	3 — Functional	4 — Mature
Decision authority	No clear governance structure; modernization decisions made ad hoc	Governance body exists; limited authority; primarily advisory	Governance body with real decision authority; meets regularly	Three-layer governance (strategic/architectural/operational) with explicit decision rights and regular cadence
Information quality	Governance receives status	Some architectural informatio	Governance-quality briefings	Systematic information translation; governance body receives analysis

	reports; no architectural context	n reaches governance; not decision-useful	prepared; architectural health reported	that informs decisions, not just activity reports
Commitment durability	Governance decisions routinely reversed under pressure; no protection mechanisms	Some governance decisions persist; significant vulnerability to reallocation	Multi-year investment commitments in place; formal process to revisit	Investment protection mechanisms active; architectural decision records maintained; commitment rationale documented for continuity
Context continuity	Institutional context lost with leadership transitions; governance starts over	Some documentation; significant context lost in transitions	Handover process for governance transitions; key context documented	Living architectural narrative maintained; formal transition process; incoming leaders briefed systematically
Strategic connection	Modernization investment not connected to strategic priorities	Loose connection; not explicitly documented or reviewed	Strategic rationale documented for major investments; reviewed annually	Explicit strategic alignment documented; governance body reviews quarterly; strategic case updated when priorities shift

Dimension 5 — Continuous Evolution

Indicator	1 — Absent	2 — Partial	3 — Functional	4 — Mature
Function structure	Modernization organized as programs; no permanent function	Partial function elements; program model still dominant	Named function with mandate and leadership; transitioning from programs	Permanent function fully established; board-level mandate; stable leadership; recognized institutional role
Funding model	All modernization investment capitalized as specific programs	Some operational elements; capital model still dominant	Operational budget for core function; capital for major initiatives	Full operational funding for core function; multi-year commitment; formal process to revisit investment level
Retrospective practice	No retrospectives; learning ad hoc or absent	Retrospectives conducted occasionally; lessons not consistently captured	Regular retrospectives with documented output; some changes to practice	Protected quarterly retrospectives; systematic learning capture; demonstrable changes to subsequent decisions

Debt recognition	Technical debt discovered reactively when it causes problems	Some debt documented; inconsistent practice	Debt recognized at creation; debt register maintained	Immediate debt recognition integrated into development workflow; sized and prioritized; debt trajectory tracked
Learning culture	Failures treated as accountability events; problems hidden; views not updated	Some learning orientation; psychological safety inconsistent	Learning culture present; retrospectives honest; some leader modeling	Strong learning culture; leaders model learning behaviors; problems surface safely; views updated openly when evidence warrants

Scoring and interpretation

Sum the scores within each dimension (maximum 20 per dimension) and record them below. Then sum the dimension scores for an overall Modernization Intelligence score (maximum 100).

Dimension	Score (max 20)	Maturity stage

Architectural Awareness		
Transformation Sequencing		
Execution Discipline		
Governance Alignment		
Continuous Evolution		
Overall MI Score (max 100)		

Score interpretation for individual dimensions: 17–20 points indicates mature, institutionalized capability in this dimension. 12–16 indicates functional capability with meaningful opportunities to improve. 7–11 indicates partial capability — the dimension exists but is not yet producing reliable value. Below 7 indicates early-stage or absent capability — this dimension is a significant gap.

Overall score interpretation: 80–100 indicates an institutionalized Modernization Intelligence organization operating at or near the top of the maturity curve. 60–79 indicates a structured organization with well-developed capability in most dimensions and specific gaps to address. 40–59 indicates a transitional organization moving from reactive toward structured — foundational capability exists but important gaps remain. Below 40 indicates a primarily reactive organization where the foundational investments in Part Two represent the near-term priority.

Building your roadmap from the assessment

The assessment produces a dimension profile — a picture of relative maturity across the five dimensions — that should directly inform the investment roadmap. Several principles guide how to use this profile to build a realistic and effective roadmap.

Address the lowest-scoring foundational dimensions first

Architectural awareness and governance alignment are foundational dimensions in the sense that low scores on either significantly constrain the value available from investing in the others. An organization with a score of 6 on architectural awareness and a score of 15 on transformation sequencing is doing sophisticated sequencing work on an inadequate information foundation — the sequencing investments are not producing their full value, and may be creating false confidence in plans that do not reflect the real state of the environment. Before investing further in sequencing sophistication, the foundational gaps in awareness should be addressed.

Similarly, an organization with strong awareness and execution capability but weak governance will find that its investments in awareness and execution do not compound over time — because the governance structures required to sustain those investments and apply them to strategic decision-making are not in place.

Look for dimension imbalances

Significant imbalances between dimension scores — where one dimension is substantially more mature than the others — are often more important signals than the overall score. An organization with a score of 18 on execution discipline and 6 on architectural awareness is executing with great discipline in directions that may not be the right ones. An organization with a score of 17 on governance alignment and 7 on continuous evolution has strong governance structures that are governing an episodic program model rather than a permanent function — the governance investment is not fully productive because the organizational model it is governing is still fundamentally incomplete.

Sequence investments to generate momentum

Maturity investments are most effective when they generate early returns that build organizational momentum and justify subsequent investments. Two investment sequencing principles apply broadly: invest first in the dimension where improvement will be most visible to senior leaders, because visible improvement builds the organizational support for continued investment. And invest early in the dimension where improvement will most directly reduce the cost or risk of the next significant modernization initiative, because cost and risk reduction is the most tangible near-term return on capability investment.

TOOL — ROADMAP PLANNING TEMPLATE

Use this template to translate assessment results into a structured capability roadmap. Complete one row for each dimension where you identified a significant gap (score below 12).

For each gap dimension: What is the current score and what score are you targeting in 12 months? What are the one or two specific practices or structures that would most directly improve the score? What does 'good' look like in concrete behavioral terms — what would you observe in the organization if the target score were achieved? Who owns the investment in this dimension? What is the resource requirement? What is the dependency relationship with other dimensions — does this investment need to precede or follow other investments?

Review the completed template with your governance body before beginning investment. The roadmap should be a governance commitment, not just a management plan — it should have the authority and the accountability mechanisms that make it more likely to be sustained than a typical planning document.

CHAPTER 12

Recognizing Your Archetype

The five recurring patterns of modernization challenge — how to identify which one describes your situation and what it means for how you approach the work

No two institutions face exactly the same modernization challenge. The specific systems, the specific dependencies, the specific organizational history, and the specific strategic context are always different. But across the many institutions that have engaged seriously with modernization, a small number of recurring structural patterns emerge — patterns that are common enough that the experience of one organization is directly relevant to another facing the same pattern, even if the technical specifics differ.

These patterns are what this chapter calls archetypes. Understanding which archetype describes your situation does not replace the specific analytical work that every modernization effort requires. But it accelerates the process of building an accurate situational picture, surfaces the most common failure modes for your specific context, and points toward the approaches that have worked for organizations in similar situations.

Most organizations will recognize elements of more than one archetype in their situation. This is normal. The archetypes are not mutually exclusive, and many institutions are navigating multiple challenges simultaneously. The value of the framework is in the clarity it provides about the primary structural challenge — the one that, if not addressed, will most significantly constrain the effectiveness of modernization work overall.

Archetype 1 — The Legacy Core Constraint

What it looks like

The Legacy Core Constraint archetype describes organizations whose most consequential operational systems — the core platforms that process transactions, manage records, or deliver primary services — are built on technology that is increasingly difficult to extend, integrate, or evolve. These systems are typically decades old, written in languages that are no longer part of the mainstream technology talent pool, running on infrastructure that is approaching end of vendor support, and tightly coupled to every other system in the environment through integrations that were built when the core system was the unquestioned center of the architecture.

The systems themselves continue to function. They are often remarkably reliable — they have been running for thirty years, they have been hardened by decades of operational experience, and they process enormous transaction volumes with consistency that newer systems often struggle to match. The problem is not that they fail. The problem is that they are increasingly difficult to change, and that the rest of the architecture has been built around them in ways that make changing anything else difficult too.

The business impact is characterized by two symptoms. The first is change velocity constraint: even small changes to the business capabilities supported by the core system are expensive and slow, because the change must be implemented in the legacy codebase and then propagated through all of the downstream systems that depend on it. The second is integration limitation: new capabilities — whether internal innovations or external partnerships — that require integration with the core system are either impossible or extremely expensive, because the core system's interfaces were not designed for the integration patterns of modern technology environments.

The primary challenge

The primary challenge in the Legacy Core Constraint archetype is not technical — it is sequencing. The core system is the most difficult system to change and the one that everything else depends on. This combination creates a sequencing paradox: you cannot modernize the periphery fully without modernizing the core, but modernizing the core is the highest-risk action in the portfolio and depends on having already built the capability and confidence that peripheral modernization provides.

Organizations that attempt to address this archetype by starting with the core — by attempting a wholesale replacement of the legacy system before building the modernization capability required to execute that replacement safely — consistently encounter the discovery problems described in Chapter Seven. The core system contains embedded institutional knowledge that is not visible from the outside, and the dependencies that surround it are denser and more complex than any pre-replacement analysis fully reveals.

The approach that works

The approach that consistently works for the Legacy Core Constraint archetype is progressive capability migration: a multi-year strategy that systematically extracts capability from the legacy core into modern platforms, leaving the core to handle what it does best — the high-volume, high-reliability transaction processing that it was built for — while surrounding it with a modern capability layer that addresses the integration and flexibility limitations.

The first investment is architectural awareness at the core: a serious, systematic analysis of what the core system actually does, at the level of business logic and embedded rules rather than just system behavior. This analysis is the most important investment in the entire Legacy Core Constraint journey, because every subsequent decision depends on accuracy about what is being preserved, what is being migrated, and what behavioral contracts must be maintained during and after migration.

The second investment is interface modernization: wrapping the legacy core with modern API interfaces that allow new capabilities to integrate with it without requiring direct integration into its legacy interfaces. This does not change what the core does — it changes how other systems communicate with it, dramatically reducing the integration barrier for new capabilities and enabling a progressive migration strategy.

The third investment, which can proceed in parallel with the second, is peripheral capability migration: systematically moving the capabilities at the edges of the core — the functions that the core performs but that could be performed by modern systems with much lower integration complexity — into purpose-built platforms. Each migration reduces the scope and complexity of the core, making subsequent migrations less risky and less expensive.

> *The Legacy Core Constraint archetype rewards patience and penalizes urgency. The organizations that navigate it most successfully are those that resist the pressure to move quickly to replacement and instead invest in the sustained, progressive approach that the complexity of the situation actually requires.*

Archetype 2 — The Integration Accumulation

What it looks like

The Integration Accumulation archetype describes organizations whose primary architectural challenge is not the age or capability of individual systems but the density and opacity of the integration layer that connects them. Individual systems may be reasonably modern and well-maintained. But the web of point-to-point integrations, middleware layers, data pipelines, and event streams that connects them has grown, over years of continuous development, into a landscape of such complexity that changes to any system carry consequences that are difficult to predict and expensive to validate.

The characteristic signature of this archetype is change risk that feels disproportionate to the scope of the changes being attempted. A simple change to a single system — adding a field, changing a response format, modifying a business rule — requires weeks of analysis and testing because the scope of downstream consequences is not known in advance. Incidents caused by integration failures are common and often surprising in their origin. And the time required to onboard engineers to the environment is long, because the integration landscape is so complex that no individual can hold a mental model of it.

The primary challenge

The primary challenge in the Integration Accumulation archetype is visibility. Unlike the Legacy Core Constraint archetype, where the primary challenge is a system that is known and understood but difficult to change, the Integration Accumulation archetype involves complexity that is largely invisible. The integrations that carry the most operational risk are often the ones that are least documented — the point-to-point connections built years ago to solve immediate problems, the middleware configurations that have accumulated exceptions over time, the behavioral dependencies that were never explicitly designed but that systems have come to rely on.

This invisibility means that the standard modernization approaches — build a target architecture, define a migration sequence, execute toward the target — consistently underestimate the complexity they will encounter. The integration landscape is not a set of known constraints to be managed. It is a partially unknown territory that must be mapped before it can be navigated.

The approach that works

The Integration Accumulation archetype requires treating integration architecture as the primary modernization domain, not as a supporting concern. The first investment is integration discovery: a systematic effort to map the actual integration landscape, using the combination of automated technical discovery and operational interview approaches described in Chapter Six. The output of this effort — a sufficiently accurate map of what integrations exist, how they are used, and what behavioral dependencies they carry — is the foundation on which all subsequent modernization decisions depend.

The second investment is integration platform rationalization: establishing a defined integration architecture — a set of standard integration patterns, a managed API platform, an event streaming infrastructure — that replaces the accumulated point-to-point complexity with a designed, governed, observable integration layer. This is not a quick initiative. It requires sustained investment over multiple years and careful migration sequencing that replaces integrations one at a time without disrupting the operational dependencies that depend on them.

The third investment is integration governance: establishing the organizational practices — integration standards, architecture review for new integrations, regular integration landscape audits — that prevent the accumulation from resuming once it has been addressed. Organizations that address Integration Accumulation without establishing integration governance typically find themselves returning to the same archetype within five to ten years.

Archetype 3 — The Platform Transition

What it looks like

The Platform Transition archetype describes organizations undertaking the migration of significant operational workloads from one technology platform to another. The most common instance is on-premises to cloud migration, but the pattern also applies to mainframe to distributed systems migration, monolith to microservices decomposition, and proprietary middleware to open standards migration. These transitions are typically motivated by compelling economic or capability rationale: cost reduction, operational flexibility, access to cloud-native capabilities, talent availability. The challenge lies in the gap between the appeal of the destination and the complexity of the journey.

The characteristic failure pattern in the Platform Transition archetype is what practitioners call lift and shift without transform: the migration of workloads to the new platform without addressing the architectural characteristics that made those workloads expensive and inflexible on the old platform. A monolithic application that was difficult to change on-premises becomes a monolithic application that is difficult to change in the cloud — at higher cost, because cloud pricing models are optimized for distributed, scalable architectures rather than for monolithic ones. The migration has occurred; the architectural improvement has not.

The primary challenge

The primary challenge in the Platform Transition archetype is scope clarity: understanding, before committing to a migration sequence, the full scope of what migration will actually require. This includes not just the technical work of moving workloads to the new platform but the architectural work of adapting those workloads to take genuine advantage of the new platform's capabilities, the dependency management work of ensuring that migrated workloads continue to function correctly in relation to the workloads that have not yet been migrated, and the organizational work of developing the skills and practices required to operate effectively on the new platform.

Each of these scope components is consistently underestimated in Platform Transition planning. The technical migration is the most visible and tends to be reasonably well scoped. The architectural adaptation is frequently deferred in favor of speed, producing the lift-and-shift failure pattern. The dependency management is frequently underestimated, because the dependency analysis required to understand migration consequences is not completed before migration commitments are made. And the organizational capability development is frequently treated as a parallel track rather than a prerequisite, producing situations where workloads are migrated to a platform that the organization does not yet know how to operate effectively.

The approach that works

Platform Transition work benefits more than almost any other archetype from investment in foundational preparation before migration begins. The foundational investments include: dependency analysis at sufficient depth to understand which workloads can be migrated independently and which require coordinated migration; pilot migration of a representative but non-critical workload to develop organizational learning about the migration process before committing to production workloads; and operational capability development — ensuring that the teams responsible for operating migrated workloads on the new platform have the training, tooling, and experience required to do so effectively before those workloads carry production load.

The migration sequence itself should be organized around dependency clusters rather than around business priority alone. Workloads that have dense dependencies with other workloads should be migrated together or in a carefully managed sequence that maintains integration continuity during the transition. And the cutover strategy — the specific approach to transitioning production traffic from old to new platform — should be incremental wherever possible, using the parallel operation and dark launch techniques described in Chapter Eight to validate behavior before full commitment.

Archetype 4 — The Regulatory Adaptation

What it looks like

The Regulatory Adaptation archetype describes organizations facing modernization requirements driven primarily by regulatory change: new data privacy requirements that mandate capabilities the current architecture cannot support, updated reporting standards that require integration and analytical infrastructure that does not exist, mandatory security controls that require architectural changes to systems that were not designed with those controls in mind, or operational requirements — such as real-time reporting, data residency, or audit trail capabilities — that legacy systems cannot meet.

The distinguishing characteristic of this archetype is external deadline pressure. Unlike the other archetypes, where the pace of modernization is determined primarily by the organization's own priorities and capacity, the Regulatory Adaptation archetype involves non-negotiable external timelines. The regulatory requirement comes into force on a specific date. The operational consequence of non-compliance — regulatory sanction, operational restriction, financial penalty — is real and significant. And the time available to achieve compliance is whatever the regulator has decided, not whatever the organization's modernization capacity allows.

The primary challenge

The primary challenge in the Regulatory Adaptation archetype is the tension between compliance urgency and architectural quality. The fastest path to compliance is often an overlay approach: building the required capability on top of or alongside existing systems without addressing the underlying architectural limitations that make those systems difficult to comply with. This approach meets the regulatory deadline but creates new forms of technical debt — the overlay capability is typically fragile, expensive to maintain, and difficult to extend when the regulatory requirements evolve further.

The slower but more durable approach is to treat regulatory adaptation as an opportunity for targeted architectural improvement: to address the compliance requirement in a way that also advances the underlying architectural quality, by building the required capability using patterns and platforms that align with the longer-term architectural direction rather than as a tactical workaround.

The approach that works

The most effective approach to Regulatory Adaptation combines short-term compliance assurance with medium-term architectural improvement. In the near term, the priority is meeting the regulatory deadline through whatever means are available, even if that means an overlay approach that creates technical debt. Non-compliance is not an acceptable outcome, and the risk of attempting a more ambitious architectural approach under deadline pressure is often higher than the risk of the technical debt that an overlay creates.

In parallel with the near-term compliance work, the medium-term planning should explicitly address the architectural limitations that made regulatory compliance difficult, and should design the follow-on work that replaces the overlay with a more architecturally sound implementation. This follow-on work should be planned and resourced before the compliance deadline is met, not after — because the window of organizational attention and regulatory urgency is open during the compliance effort and tends to close once compliance is achieved.

Archetype 5 — The Institutional Learning

What it looks like

The Institutional Learning archetype describes organizations that have been through significant modernization experiences — sometimes successful, sometimes not — and are in the process of developing better organizational capability for the work ahead. These organizations have direct experience with some or all of the failure patterns described in Chapter Four. They have invested in transformation programs that did not produce the durable improvement they were intended to produce. They have experienced the discovery gap, the governance failure, or the completion fallacy in operational reality rather than in theory.

What distinguishes this archetype from the others is not the technical character of the modernization challenge but the organizational starting point. The institution has accumulated real learning about modernization from its own experience — knowledge about what does not work and what the failure patterns look like in practice. The challenge is translating that experiential learning into organizational capability: building the structures, practices, and habits that allow the institution to do modernization better going forward rather than repeating the same patterns with incrementally better execution.

The primary challenge

The primary challenge in the Institutional Learning archetype is organizational inertia. The patterns that did not work — the program model, the replacement default, the episodic investment cycle — are embedded in organizational structures, budget processes, governance expectations, and cultural norms that resist change. The people who have experienced the failure patterns know, at some level, that a different approach is needed. But the organizational machinery that surrounds them continues to produce the same approach.

The inertia is not malicious. The people who continue to organize modernization as programs, to fund it through capital appropriations, and to treat it as an episodic activity are not acting in bad faith. They are acting within the structures and incentives that their organizations have established. Changing those structures and incentives is the primary challenge, and it requires the organizational design work described in Chapter Ten — the transition from program to function, the funding model change, the governance redesign — more than it requires any specific technical modernization approach.

The approach that works

The approach that works for the Institutional Learning archetype is honest organizational diagnosis followed by deliberate structural change. The diagnosis requires being explicit about what has not worked and why — naming the failure patterns, connecting them to the structural causes described in this book, and building the shared organizational understanding that a structural change is required rather than better execution of the same approach.

The structural change requires the specific transitions described in Chapter Ten: building the case for a permanent modernization function, piloting the function model in a bounded domain, demonstrating its value through specific evidence, and using that evidence to build the organizational support for broader transition. This is a multi-year effort, and it requires the organizational patience and leadership commitment that Chapter Nine describes. But for organizations in the Institutional Learning archetype, it is the only path that produces genuinely different outcomes.

DIAGNOSTIC — IDENTIFYING YOUR PRIMARY ARCHETYPE

The following questions help identify the archetype that most closely describes your primary modernization challenge. Answer each question as specifically as possible, based on the actual operational experience of your organization.

When modernization initiatives have encountered unexpected complexity or cost, where has that complexity typically originated? If the answer is in the systems being replaced or migrated, Legacy Core Constraint is likely primary. If it is in the integrations between systems, Integration Accumulation is likely primary. If it is in the migration process itself, Platform Transition may be primary.

What is the primary driver of modernization investment in your organization — operational constraint, platform transition economics, regulatory requirement, or organizational learning from previous experience? The primary driver often points directly to the primary archetype.

When you think about the modernization work that would have the highest impact on your organization's strategic options over the next three years, what is the primary barrier to doing it? Systems that cannot be changed? Integration complexity that makes all changes risky? A regulatory deadline that is consuming capacity? Or organizational structures and habits that continue to produce episodic programs rather than continuous improvement?

Your answers to these questions should point toward one archetype as primary. The path forward in Chapter Twelve is to use the approach described for your primary archetype as the organizing principle for your modernization strategy, while recognizing that elements of other archetypes may also need to be addressed.

CHAPTER 13

AI as a Modernization Tool

What AI capabilities genuinely help with in modernization work, where they fall short, and how to integrate them into a Modernization Intelligence framework without misunderstanding what they can and cannot do

No serious treatment of software modernization written in the mid-2020s can avoid the question of AI. The capabilities of large language models and AI-powered development tools have advanced rapidly enough that their potential relevance to modernization work is real and worth examining carefully. They have also been marketed with enough enthusiasm that separating genuine capability from promotional optimism requires some analytical effort.

This chapter provides a clear-eyed assessment of where AI tools genuinely help in modernization work, where they do not, and how to integrate them into the Modernization Intelligence framework in ways that amplify the framework's effectiveness without creating false confidence in capabilities that AI tools do not actually have. The organizing principle is the distinction that runs through this entire book: Modernization Intelligence is an organizational capability. AI tools can amplify the productivity of the people who hold that capability. They cannot substitute for it.

What AI actually is in this context

The AI tools relevant to modernization work in the current environment fall into three main categories, each with distinct capabilities and distinct limitations.

Large language models are general-purpose text and code generation systems that can be applied to a wide range of modernization-related tasks: analyzing codebases, generating documentation, answering questions about unfamiliar code, translating between programming languages, and assisting with the writing tasks that modernization work generates. Their capabilities in these areas are real and have advanced significantly. Their limitations are also real: they generate outputs that can be plausible without being accurate, they do not have genuine understanding of the institutional context in which modernization work occurs, and their outputs require human review and judgment to be safely applied.

AI-powered code analysis tools use machine learning techniques to analyze codebases at scale: identifying patterns, detecting potential vulnerabilities, mapping dependencies, and surfacing complexity indicators. These tools can process codebases far larger than any human analyst could review in detail, and they can identify patterns and dependencies that human review might miss. Their limitations lie in the interpretation layer: the tool can identify that a particular code pattern exists and flag it as potentially significant, but the judgment about whether it is actually significant in a specific architectural and operational context requires human expertise.

AI-powered code transformation tools use machine learning to automate specific categories of code change: language migration, API modernization, test generation, and refactoring. These tools have demonstrated genuine productivity improvements in controlled contexts, particularly for the routine and rule-bound transformations that consume significant engineering time in modernization work. Their limitations are in the handling of complex, context-dependent cases: the transformations that require judgment about business logic, operational behavior, or architectural intent are the transformations that AI tools handle least reliably.

Where AI genuinely helps in modernization work

Accelerating architectural discovery

The architectural discovery work described in Chapter Six — the systems inventory, dependency mapping, and operational behavior documentation that form the foundation of architectural awareness — is among the most time-consuming and labor-intensive work in the Modernization Intelligence discipline. AI-powered code analysis tools can accelerate this work substantially.

In the specific context of dependency mapping, AI tools can analyze large codebases to identify integration patterns, database access patterns, and API calls that might not be visible from architecture documentation alone. A codebase analysis that would require weeks of manual review can be completed by AI tools in hours, producing an initial dependency map that human analysts can then validate and extend with the behavioral and organizational dependencies that automated tools cannot detect.

The productivity impact of this acceleration is significant: it reduces the time and cost required to achieve the level of architectural awareness that effective modernization demands, making the foundational investment more accessible to organizations that might otherwise defer it because of cost. The caveat is important: AI-generated dependency maps are starting points, not finished products. The quality of the map depends on the quality of the codebase analysis, which in turn depends on the completeness of the codebase access provided to the tool and on the accuracy of the tool's pattern recognition. Human validation remains essential.

Reducing low-judgment transformation work

A significant proportion of the engineering effort in most modernization programs goes to transformation work that is routine in character: converting code from one language to another, updating API call patterns to conform to new interface standards, generating boilerplate that reflects established patterns, updating test suites to cover changed functionality. This work is necessary but not intellectually demanding — it is the kind of work that experienced engineers find tedious and that creates execution bottlenecks when the volume of required changes is large.

AI-powered code transformation tools can automate substantial portions of this work, freeing engineering capacity for the judgment-intensive work that determines transformation quality. In language migration projects — COBOL to Java, for example, or Java to Kotlin — AI transformation tools have demonstrated the ability to handle the majority of routine translation work, leaving human engineers to address the cases where business logic, performance characteristics, or operational behavior requires careful consideration.

The practical benefit is not just cost reduction. It is also risk reduction: when the routine transformation work is automated and human attention is concentrated on the judgment-intensive cases, the overall quality of transformation output tends to improve, because the cases most likely to contain errors — the complex, context-dependent ones — are the ones that receive the most careful human review.

Supporting documentation and knowledge capture

The knowledge capture work described in Chapter Ten — the practice of systematically converting tacit architectural knowledge into explicit organizational knowledge — is labor-intensive and often deferred when execution pressure is high. AI tools can reduce the friction of this work in several ways.

Large language models can assist with the generation of architectural documentation from existing code and system artifacts: producing first-draft descriptions of system behavior, integration patterns, and data flows that human architects can then review, correct, and augment with the contextual knowledge that automated analysis cannot capture. This reduces the time required to produce useful documentation from scratch, which is often the primary barrier to documentation work being done consistently.

AI tools can also assist with the retrospective knowledge capture process: analyzing retrospective notes and incident records to identify patterns, synthesize lessons, and generate structured learning documents that capture the key insights from operational experience. This does not replace the human judgment required to interpret and apply those lessons, but it reduces the administrative burden of the knowledge capture process.

Where AI does not help — and where it misleads

Strategic judgment

The strategic dimensions of Modernization Intelligence — determining the architectural direction that best serves institutional strategic priorities, evaluating the trade-offs between competing modernization approaches, deciding which initiatives to invest in and in what sequence — are not tasks that AI tools can perform. They require the combination of technical knowledge, organizational understanding, and strategic context that constitutes the core capability of the modernization function. AI tools can provide information that informs these judgments. They cannot make them.

This limitation is particularly important to understand because AI tools can generate outputs that appear authoritative on strategic questions. A large language model asked to recommend a modernization sequence will produce a recommendation that reads confidently and coherently. It will not be grounded in accurate knowledge of the institution's specific environment, strategic context, or organizational constraints. Using AI-generated strategic recommendations without the human judgment required to evaluate them against institutional reality is one of the more consequential ways that AI tools can mislead in the modernization context.

Organizational capability

The organizational dimensions of Modernization Intelligence — the governance structures, the institutional habits, the leadership engagement, the cultural change required to treat modernization as a continuous function — are entirely beyond the scope of AI tools. No current or foreseeable AI system can build the coalition required to sustain modernization investment, navigate the political dynamics that governance design involves, develop the learning culture that makes retrospectives productive, or maintain the organizational relationships that make complex change possible.

The risk of misunderstanding this limitation is not primarily that organizations will expect AI tools to do organizational work directly. The risk is more subtle: that the productivity gains from AI tools in technical work will create an impression that the organizational work is less necessary — that if the technical work can be automated, the overall modernization challenge is more tractable than it actually is. This impression is false and dangerous. The technical work that AI tools can accelerate is important. The organizational work that they cannot touch is more important. Accelerating the former while neglecting the latter produces technically sophisticated modernization programs that fail for organizational reasons.

Accuracy in complex systems

AI tools operate by pattern recognition: they identify patterns in training data and apply those patterns to new inputs. This approach works well for tasks where the relevant patterns are well-represented in training data and where the cost of errors is low. It works less well for tasks where the relevant patterns are highly specific to an institutional context that is not represented in training data, or where errors carry significant operational consequences.

In the modernization context, this limitation is most significant in the areas of behavioral dependency identification and business logic extraction from legacy code. AI tools can identify code patterns that might indicate behavioral dependencies or embedded business logic. They cannot reliably determine whether a specific pattern is operationally significant in a specific institutional context, or whether a specific piece of business logic is critical to operational correctness. These determinations require the institutional knowledge and operational experience that human architects and engineers possess and that AI tools do not.

Integrating AI tools into the Modernization Intelligence framework

The practical question for most modernization leaders is not whether AI tools are valuable in the abstract but how to integrate them into a specific organizational context in ways that produce genuine productivity improvement without creating the false confidence or misapplied effort that AI limitations can produce.

Three integration principles apply across contexts. First, use AI tools to accelerate work that is already well-understood and well-scoped, not to scope or understand work that is not yet defined. AI discovery tools should be applied after the scope of a dependency analysis has been defined, not used as a substitute for the human judgment required to define that scope. AI transformation tools should be applied to code that has been analyzed and understood, not used to transform code whose behavioral characteristics have not been established.

Second, treat AI outputs as inputs to human judgment, not as outputs ready for use. Every significant output from an AI tool in the modernization context — a dependency map, a transformed codebase, a documentation draft — requires human review before it is used in consequential decisions. The review should be calibrated to the stakes: a documentation draft that will be used for internal reference requires less rigorous review than a transformed codebase that will be deployed to production. But the review step should never be eliminated.

Third, track and evaluate AI tool contribution separately from overall modernization progress. Understanding which aspects of modernization work AI tools are genuinely accelerating, and which aspects are still primarily dependent on human effort, provides the evidence base required to make good decisions about where to invest in AI tool capability and where to invest in human capability development.

LEADERSHIP NOTE — EVALUATING AI TOOL CLAIMS IN MODERNIZATION

As AI capabilities in software development continue to advance, the market for AI modernization tools will grow, and the claims made by vendors in this space will be difficult to evaluate without a clear framework. The following questions provide a starting point for evaluating any AI modernization tool claim.

What specific task does this tool perform, and what is the scope of that task relative to the overall modernization challenge? A tool that accelerates one specific category of work — even significantly — may have limited impact on overall modernization effectiveness if that category is not a primary bottleneck.

What human judgment is still required to use this tool's outputs effectively? The most important question about any AI tool is not what it can do but what it cannot do — because the gaps define the human capability investment required to use the tool safely.

What is the evidence base for the tool's claimed productivity improvement? Vendor demonstrations on representative samples rarely capture the full complexity of real institutional environments. Pilot deployments in your own environment, with your own systems, are the most reliable evidence.

How does this tool's capability interact with the organizational dimensions of the modernization challenge? Tools that accelerate technical work without supporting the organizational capability development required for continuous evolution may produce short-term productivity gains that do not compound into sustained architectural improvement.

CHAPTER 14

Building Your Modernization Function

The organizational design, the internal case, the hiring approach, and the first-year roadmap for establishing a permanent modernization capability in your institution

---

Every chapter in this book has been building toward this one. The framework is clear. The failure patterns are understood. The maturity assessment has produced a picture of where your organization currently stands. The archetype analysis has identified the primary structural challenge. The governance and continuous evolution chapters have described the organizational design that makes the capability permanent. Now comes the question that determines whether any of that knowledge produces organizational change: how do you actually build the modernization function?

This chapter is a practical guide to that question. It works through the organizational design decisions in sequence: how to make the internal case that gets the function authorized and funded, how to design the function's structure, how to hire and develop the team, how to establish the governance relationships that give the function organizational authority, and what the first year of operation should look like. It is written for the person who has been given the responsibility of building this capability and needs a concrete plan for how to proceed.

Making the internal case

Before the modernization function can be built, it must be authorized. Authorization requires making the case to the leaders who have the power to create the function, fund it, and protect it through the competing pressures that will arise. This is not primarily a technical communication challenge. It is an organizational influence challenge, and it requires the same kind of strategic preparation that any significant organizational investment requires.

Understanding your audience

The leaders whose support is essential vary by organizational context, but in most institutions they include the CEO or equivalent executive leader, the CFO, and the board or its technology oversight committee. Each of these audiences has different motivations, different risk orientations, and different frames for evaluating the case you are making.

The CEO's primary concern is strategic: does this investment make the organization more capable of executing its strategy? The case for the modernization function that resonates with a CEO is the strategic optionality argument: the specific strategic initiatives that the current architectural condition is constraining, and the specific capabilities that a functioning modernization discipline would enable. Abstract arguments about technical debt do not move CEOs. Concrete connections to strategic priorities do.

The CFO's primary concern is economic: is this a sound use of institutional resources? The case that resonates with a CFO is the cost and risk argument: the specific cost of the current approach — the maintenance burden, the rework costs, the manual compensation costs described in Chapter Three — and the expected trajectory of that cost if the current approach continues. CFOs respond to trend analysis: if maintenance as a proportion of technology investment has increased from forty percent to sixty percent over the past five years, the projection of that trend over the next five years is a powerful argument for structural change.

The board's primary concern is fiduciary: is the organization managing its technology risk appropriately? The case that resonates with a board is the risk argument: the operational, regulatory, and strategic risks that accumulating architectural debt creates, and the governance case for establishing a permanent function with board-level visibility and accountability. Boards that have experience with technology-related organizational failures — and most boards of mature institutions have some — are receptive to the argument that architecture deserves the same systematic organizational attention as financial risk or operational risk.

Building the evidence base

The most persuasive internal cases are grounded in specific institutional evidence rather than in general arguments about modernization. Before making the case, invest in the analysis required to produce specific, credible numbers: the maintenance burden calculation, the delayed delivery cost estimate, the manual compensation inventory, and the foregone opportunity assessment described in Chapter Three. These numbers will be approximate — they cannot be precise — but they should be defensible, with documented assumptions and honest uncertainty ranges.

The evidence base should also include the organizational history: a clear-eyed account of what previous modernization programs have and have not produced, why the outcomes fell short of the investment, and what the structural reasons are for those outcomes. This is not a blame exercise — it is a diagnosis of the structural conditions that a different organizational approach would address. Presenting this diagnosis honestly, without minimizing the past investment or overpromising the future returns, builds the credibility that the internal case requires.

The ask

The internal case should culminate in a specific, concrete ask: not a vague request for support for modernization, but a specific proposal for the organizational structure, the initial investment level, and the governance commitments that the modernization function requires. The specificity of the ask signals the seriousness of the proposal and gives the decision-making leaders something concrete to approve, modify, or reject.

The initial ask should be calibrated to what is organizationally achievable in a first step. For most organizations, the most credible first ask is not for the full permanent function described in Chapter Ten but for the pilot described there: a defined domain, a defined team, a defined budget, and a defined evaluation period at the end of which the evidence produced by the pilot will inform a decision about broader expansion. This approach reduces the risk for the decision-making leaders and builds the evidence base required for the broader commitment.

Designing the function structure

Once the function has been authorized, the first organizational task is designing its structure: the roles, responsibilities, reporting relationships, and governance connections that define how the function operates.

The minimum viable structure

For most organizations in the early stages of building a modernization function, the minimum viable structure consists of three roles: a function leader, an architectural intelligence lead, and an execution lead. This is not a complete organization — it is the core around which the full function will be built — but it is sufficient to begin the foundational work of building architectural awareness, establishing governance relationships, and executing initial transformation work.

The function leader is the most critical hire. This is the person who will make the internal case for the function's value, build the relationships with senior leaders that give the function organizational authority, represent the function in governance conversations, and set the cultural tone that determines whether the function develops the learning orientation and organizational effectiveness it requires. The talent profile described in Chapter Ten — deep technical knowledge, strategic judgment, organizational fluency, and communication skill — applies most fully to this role. Do not compromise on it.

The architectural intelligence lead is responsible for building and maintaining the architectural awareness that is the function's information foundation. This is a technically demanding role that requires deep knowledge of the institution's specific environment — the systems, the integrations, the operational behaviors, the history. It is typically best filled by an internal appointment: someone who already has the institutional knowledge that the role requires, developed through years of working in the environment. If the person exists internally, promote them. If they do not, the role can be filled externally, but the time to institutional effectiveness will be longer.

The execution lead is responsible for leading the transformation work that the function prioritizes. This is a program leadership role that requires both technical credibility and organizational effectiveness: the ability to assemble and direct the execution teams, manage the dependencies and risks that emerge during implementation, and maintain the execution discipline described in Chapter Eight across complex, multi-workstream delivery programs.

The extended network

Beyond the core team, the modernization function operates through an extended network of capability that it coordinates but does not own. This network includes the domain architects and technical leads embedded in business units who provide local architectural knowledge and execution capacity, the external specialists who provide expertise for specific transformation challenges, the operational teams whose engagement is essential for executing changes to the systems they run, and the governance participants whose authority and strategic perspective give the function's work organizational legitimacy.

Managing this extended network effectively is one of the most important and most challenging aspects of the function leader role. The network members do not report to the function leader, and the function cannot direct their work through organizational authority. It can only influence through the quality of its analysis, the relevance of its insights to their work, and the organizational relationships that the function leader builds over time. Building these relationships is a long-term investment, and it should be treated as such from the function's first days.

Governance positioning

The organizational positioning of the modernization function within the governance structure is a significant design decision that affects the function's authority, visibility, and ability to influence decisions at the appropriate level. The function should have a direct reporting relationship to a senior leader — the CTO, the COO, or the CEO depending on organizational context — who has the authority to defend the function's mandate and investment level when they are challenged. A modernization function that reports to a middle-level IT manager does not have the organizational positioning required to influence the strategic decisions that the function's work depends on.

The function leader should also have a defined role in the governance structures described in Chapter Nine: a seat at the architectural governance table, access to the strategic governance body, and the organizational authority to escalate issues that require executive-level decision. Without this governance positioning, the function is advisory rather than operational — it can produce analysis and recommendations, but it cannot drive the decisions and investments that architectural improvement requires.

Hiring and developing the team

The quality of the modernization function is ultimately determined by the quality of the people in it. This section provides specific guidance on the hiring approach and the development investments that build the team capability the function requires.

The hiring approach

Hiring for the modernization function is different from hiring for a standard technology role, because the talent profile is unusual in ways that standard job descriptions and standard interview processes are not designed to surface. The combination of technical depth, strategic judgment, organizational fluency, and learning orientation that effective modernization requires is rare, and the standard technology hiring process — which typically focuses on technical skill assessment through coding exercises and system design interviews — will not reliably identify it.

Effective hiring for the modernization function requires interview processes that explicitly assess the non-technical dimensions of the profile. Ask candidates to describe a modernization or transformation challenge they have navigated and what they learned from it — the quality of the reflection tells you more about strategic judgment and learning orientation than any technical assessment. Ask them to describe a governance or organizational challenge that affected technical work and how they addressed it — this surfaces organizational effectiveness in ways that technical questions cannot. And ask them to explain a complex technical trade-off in terms that a non-technical executive could understand — this tests the communication skill that the function requires without requiring the candidate to pretend they are in an executive meeting.

For the function leader role specifically, behavioral reference checks with people who have worked with the candidate in complex organizational environments — not just technical colleagues but people who have seen them navigate governance, build coalitions, and sustain organizational commitment through competing pressures — are among the most valuable inputs to the hiring decision.

Development investments

Even the best hires will have gaps relative to the full modernization function talent profile. A technically excellent architectural intelligence lead may need development in strategic communication. An organizationally effective execution lead may need development in architectural analysis. Identifying and investing in these development gaps from the function's early days is important, both for the quality of the function's work and for the retention of talented people who value growth.

The most valuable development investments for modernization function team members are typically those that expand exposure rather than deepen existing expertise. Rotations into governance conversations that team members do not normally participate in. Structured exposure to the strategic planning process and how architectural decisions connect to it. Relationships with senior leaders in domains outside the team member's direct experience. These exposure investments build the organizational fluency and strategic context that makes technical expertise more useful in the modernization context.

The first year

The first year of a new modernization function is critically important: it establishes the organizational credibility, the stakeholder relationships, and the institutional habits that will determine the function's effectiveness for years to come. It also sets the cultural tone and the expectations of quality that the function will carry forward. Getting the first year right is worth significant deliberate attention.

The first ninety days: establish the foundation

The first priority in the first ninety days is not producing transformation deliverables — it is building the information foundation and the organizational relationships required to produce good transformation decisions. The function leader should spend this period conducting the architectural discovery described in Chapter Six, meeting with senior leaders across the organization to understand their perspectives on the modernization challenge, and establishing the governance relationships described in Chapter Nine.

The architectural discovery work in this period serves two purposes. First, it produces the foundational knowledge that all subsequent modernization decisions depend on. Second, and less obviously, it builds organizational credibility: the function leader who can describe the institution's actual architectural condition — with specific, accurate knowledge of the systems, the dependencies, and the operational risks — commands the respect of the technical leaders whose cooperation the function will need. Generic knowledge of architecture and modernization is expected. Specific knowledge of this institution's environment is rare and valuable.

The governance relationship work in this period is equally important. The function leader should meet with each member of the strategic governance body to understand their priorities, their current understanding of the architectural situation, and their expectations for what the modernization function will produce. These conversations are not briefings — they are relationship-building conversations in which the function leader is learning as much as they are informing. The governance participants who feel that the function leader understands their priorities and takes their perspectives seriously are far more likely to be engaged governance participants than those who feel they are receiving technical updates from a function they do not fully understand.

Days ninety through one-eighty: execute a visible win

The second priority, which should begin in earnest after the foundational work of the first ninety days, is executing a visible win: a specific modernization initiative that produces clear, attributable operational improvement within the first six months of the function's operation. The purpose of this early win is not primarily the operational improvement itself — though that is valuable — it is the organizational credibility that demonstrable early success builds.

The early win should be chosen carefully. It should be genuinely high-value, not cosmetic. It should be achievable within the first six months, which means it should be bounded in scope and low in dependency complexity. And it should be visible to the senior leaders whose continued support the function requires: connected to a strategic priority they care about, or producing operational improvement in an area they have previously identified as a concern.

Delivering the early win requires applying the execution discipline described in Chapter Eight from the function's first active initiative. The quality of execution in the first visible initiative sets the institutional expectation for how the function works and what standard of discipline it maintains. This is not the moment to cut corners in the interest of speed.

Days one-eighty through three-sixty: establish the rhythm

By the end of the first year, the modernization function should have established the operating rhythm that will carry it forward: the governance calendar with its quarterly, monthly, and weekly cadences; the retrospective practice that makes the function a learning organization; the architectural awareness maintenance practices that keep the information foundation current; and the sequencing and roadmapping function that translates awareness into plans.

The end-of-year assessment should evaluate the function against the Modernization Intelligence Maturity Assessment from Chapter Eleven. The score at the end of year one will not be high — building genuine capability takes longer than a year — but the trajectory should be clearly positive, and the specific gaps that remain should inform the investment priorities for year two. This assessment, presented to the governance body with honest interpretation and a specific investment proposal for the coming year, is both a governance accountability mechanism and a communication of the function's value. It demonstrates that the function is measuring itself against the outcomes it was created to produce, not just against the activities it has completed.

TOOL — MODERNIZATION FUNCTION CHARTER TEMPLATE

The function charter is the founding document that defines the function's mandate, scope, governance relationships, and success criteria. It should be endorsed by the executive sponsor before the function begins operation. A strong charter provides the organizational authority the function needs and the accountability framework that makes governance oversight meaningful.
Mandate: One to two sentences that define the function's core organizational responsibility. Example: 'The Modernization function is responsible for building and sustaining the institutional capability to continuously evolve the organization's software architecture in alignment with strategic priorities, maintaining the architectural quality required for operational effectiveness and strategic adaptability.'
Scope: A clear definition of the systems, domains, and initiatives that fall within the function's responsibility, and the boundaries of its authority relative to other technology functions.
Governance relationships: The function's position in the governance structure — reporting relationship, membership in governance bodies, authority to escalate issues, relationship with architecture and IT functions.
Success criteria: The specific outcome metrics against which the function's effectiveness will be evaluated: technical debt trajectory, change velocity, disruption rate, and strategic capability enablement. Include the measurement approach and the reporting cadence.
Investment commitment: The initial budget commitment, the funding model (operational or capital), and the process for reviewing and adjusting investment level at defined intervals.
Review mechanism: How and when the function's charter will be reviewed — annually is typical, with an extraordinary review available if strategic priorities shift significantly.

TOOL — FIRST-YEAR MODERNIZATION FUNCTION ROADMAP

Use this template to plan the key activities and milestones for the function's first year of operation.

Days 1–90 (Foundation): Complete systems inventory for the primary domain. Complete dependency mapping for core systems. Establish governance calendar and attend first cycle of each governance layer. Meet with all key stakeholders. Produce initial architectural health baseline. Identify early win candidate.
Days 90–180 (Early Win): Select and scope the early win initiative. Complete execution readiness assessment. Execute the early win using the incremental delivery approach. Validate outcomes against expectations. Communicate results to governance body and key stakeholders.
Days 180–270 (Rhythm Establishment): Conduct first formal retrospective. Establish architectural debt recognition practice. Begin continuous discovery rotation. Update transformation roadmap based on first-half learning. Present mid-year maturity assessment to governance body.
Days 270–365 (Year-End Assessment): Complete year-end maturity assessment across all five MI dimensions. Present assessment and year-two investment proposal to governance body. Document institutional learning from year one. Update function charter if warranted. Plan team development investments for year two.

END OF PART THREE

Part Three has brought the Modernization Intelligence framework into organizational practice. Chapter Eleven provided the diagnostic tools for understanding where your organization currently stands across all five dimensions and how to build a realistic roadmap from that position. Chapter Twelve provided the archetype framework for recognizing the primary structural character of your modernization challenge and the approaches that work best for each. Chapter Thirteen examined AI tools with the clear-eyed assessment they deserve — as genuine amplifiers of human capability in specific categories of work, not as substitutes for the organizational capability that Modernization Intelligence represents. Chapter Fourteen provided the practical guide to building the modernization function itself: making the case, designing the structure, hiring the team, positioning the function in governance, and executing the first year.

What remains is the conclusion: the final institutional argument for why this work matters, why it is worth the sustained investment it requires, and what the organizations that make that investment can expect to achieve. The conclusion is written not as inspiration but as a statement of organizational reality — the kind of plain-spoken authority that the challenge deserves and that the readers of this book, who have committed the time to work through it, have earned.

CONCLUSION

The Institutional Argument

This book has made a sustained argument. It has described the structural reality of modern institutional software environments with enough specificity that the complexity is visible rather than abstract. It has connected that complexity to the economic and strategic costs that organizations absorb when they manage it inadequately. It has examined the structural reasons that traditional modernization approaches have fallen short — not because of poor execution but because the organizational model has been wrong. And it has worked through a framework for a different organizational model: Modernization Intelligence, the institutional capability that allows continuous architectural evolution to proceed as a permanent discipline rather than a recurring crisis.

What remains is to state the institutional argument directly — without the qualification that comes from building it carefully, without the hedging that comes from presenting a framework rather than a conclusion. The argument deserves to be stated plainly.

What is actually at stake

Software architecture is now a primary determinant of institutional performance. This is not a technology trend. It is a structural shift in how consequential institutional work gets done. The organizations that deliver services, fulfill obligations, execute strategies, and respond to changing demands do all of this through software systems. The condition of those systems — how well they can support the work that needs to be done, how quickly they can be adapted when that work changes, how reliably they operate under the demands placed on them — is a primary input to institutional effectiveness.

This shift has been underway for decades, but its implications have not been fully absorbed into how institutions are led and governed. Software architecture is still largely treated as a technical concern — something managed within the technology function and reported upward in the form of project status and IT budget. The executives who are responsible for institutional strategy and institutional performance still, in most organizations, lack the frameworks and the language to engage with architectural condition as the strategic variable it has become.

The consequence is predictable and visible. Institutions that should be able to respond quickly to regulatory changes cannot, because their systems require months to modify. Institutions that should be able to integrate with partner ecosystems cannot, because their integration infrastructure was not designed for the integration patterns those partnerships require. Institutions that should be able to capitalize on new capabilities — in AI, in cloud services, in data analytics — find that capitalizing on them requires architectural work that their current environments cannot support without disruption. The architecture is constraining the institution, and the institution does not have the organizational framework to address that constraint at the level it actually operates.

What Modernization Intelligence provides

Modernization Intelligence is the organizational framework that addresses this gap. It does not promise that architectural evolution is easy — it is not. It does not promise that building the capability is fast — it is not. What it provides is a principled, structured approach to turning what has historically been a recurring crisis into a managed organizational function.

The five dimensions of the framework — architectural awareness, transformation sequencing, execution discipline, governance alignment, and continuous evolution — address the five most consistent structural failure points in institutional modernization. They are not independently useful. They are a system, and the system produces compounding returns over time that no dimension can produce on its own. Each year of investment in the full system builds the capability for the next year more effectively than the year before. Each cycle of modernization work generates institutional knowledge that reduces the cost and risk of subsequent cycles. Each improvement in architectural quality expands the range of operational and strategic options available to the institution.

This compounding dynamic is the most important economic characteristic of Modernization Intelligence, and it is the characteristic most consistently underappreciated in investment decision-making. Institutions that invest in the capability for three years have a more effective modernization function than institutions that have invested for one year, not just in proportion to the additional investment but because of the accumulation of knowledge, relationship, and organizational habit that three years of continuous operation produces. Institutions that invest for ten years have capabilities that simply cannot be purchased in a single program cycle at any price. The capability compounds, and the compounding is the point.

> *Modernization is no longer an improvement initiative. It is a defining condition of institutional effectiveness.*

The choice that is available now

The organizations reading this book are at different points on the maturity curve. Some are primarily reactive, addressing architectural constraint when it becomes acute and returning to other priorities when the immediate pressure subsides. Some are structured, executing modernization programs with reasonable reliability but still organized around the episodic model that produces the completion fallacy. Some are beginning the transition toward institutionalized capability, with some elements of the framework in place and others still to be built.

For every organization, regardless of current position, the choice is the same: continue on the current trajectory, or invest in the structural changes required to compound capability over time. The current trajectory is not neutral. Architectural complexity accumulates. Technical debt grows faster than it is retired when there is no sustained investment in retiring it. The cost of modernization rises as the environment ages and as the technical expertise required to navigate it becomes scarcer. Organizations on the current trajectory are not standing still — they are moving, slowly, toward a more constrained and more expensive future.

The investment required to change this trajectory is real and not trivial. It requires organizational design changes that challenge established structures. It requires funding model changes that challenge established budget conventions. It requires governance changes that challenge established leadership habits. It requires the institutional patience to invest in capability development through a period when the returns are not yet fully visible. None of these requirements is modest.

But the investment is available to be made now. The framework exists. The practices are documented. The diagnostic tools are in hand. The organizational case — the economic argument, the strategic argument, the governance argument — is clear. What remains is the organizational will to make the structural commitments that translate understanding into capability.

The institutions that make those commitments will find, over time, that architectural evolution becomes a source of institutional strength rather than a recurring crisis. They will find that their technology environments support their strategic ambitions rather than constraining them. They will find that modernization is simply part of how they manage their organizations — no more exceptional than financial management, no more discretionary than operational excellence.

That is the institution that Modernization Intelligence is designed to build. And it begins with the decision to start.

Modernization is no longer an improvement initiative. It is a defining condition of institutional effectiveness.

REFERENCE TOOLKIT

All Frameworks, Tools & Checklists

This section consolidates every diagnostic tool, assessment framework, decision checklist, and planning template from the book into a single reference. Tools are organized by chapter and labeled by type. Each is designed to be used directly — in leadership conversations, team assessments, and planning sessions — without requiring the reader to locate it within the chapter context from which it came.

Where a tool references scoring or interpretation guidance from the chapter, a brief reminder is included. Where a tool is a template to be completed, blank space is provided for notes.

Part I Tools — Diagnosing the Challenge

Tool 1.1 — Is architecture a strategic conversation? (Ch. 1)

Use this before engaging leadership on modernization investment. A diagnostic for assessing whether the organizational conditions for a strategic modernization conversation exist.

Question	Current situation	Gap / opportunity

Does your executive committee have shared language for architectural condition and its strategic implications, or does conversation stay at project status and IT budget level?		
When major strategic initiatives are planned, does the discussion explicitly address whether the current architecture can support them, and at what cost and timeline?		
Is there a senior leader with both technical credibility and organizational authority to address architecture at the strategic level? Are they in the right governance conversations?		
When modernization programs have been undertaken, have they produced durable improvement in architectural condition, or has the environment gradually returned to		

its prior state within a few years?		

Tool 1.2 — Environmental Clarity Assessment (Ch. 2)

Rate each question 1 (no reliable answer) to 4 (current, accurate, widely shared answer). Score 16–20: strong foundation. Score 10–15: significant gaps. Below 10: discovery should be immediate priority.

Question	Score (1–4)	Notes
Can you identify all production systems, including shadow IT and locally maintained tools carrying real operational load?		
Do you have a current dependency map including implicit behavioral dependencies, not just formally documented APIs?		
Do you know which systems, if unavailable for 24 hours, would cause the most significant operational impact?		
When a change is proposed to a core		

system, do you have reliable mechanisms for assessing downstream effects before implementation?		
Is your architectural documentation current enough to be useful for modernization planning?		

Tool 1.3 — Architectural Friction Cost Framework (Ch. 3)

Four steps to estimating the cost of architectural constraint for internal investment decision-making.

Step	Activity	Your estimate	Assumptions
1	Quantify the maintenance burden gap: what proportion of technology spend goes to maintenance vs. new capability? Compare to a target of 40% maintenance / 60% new capability. Excess above target = conservative		

	direct friction cost estimate.		
2	Catalog and cost delayed deliveries: review the past 2–3 years for projects significantly delayed vs. original estimates. Estimate the business cost of each delay in revenue, compliance, or service quality terms.		
3	Inventory manual compensations: survey operational departments for manual processes that compensate for integration gaps or system limitations. Estimate annual staff cost for each.		
4	Identify foregone strategic opportunities:		

	review past strategic discussions for options declined or constrained by architectural concerns. Make rough estimates of foregone value.		

Tool 1.4 — Five Failure Patterns Self-Assessment (Ch. 4)

Rate your organization's exposure to each failure pattern 1 (low) to 5 (high).

Pattern	What to look for	Exposure (1–5)	Key evidence in your organization
Program model	Modernization organized as bounded projects; no permanent function; investment discontinued between programs		
Replacement default	Legacy systems routinely targeted for wholesale replacement; discovery work underinvested;		

	cutover treated as an event		
Governance failure	Leadership transitions have reversed architectural decisions; annual planning creates vulnerability to investment reallocation		
Discovery gap	Significant undiscovered dependencies routinely found during implementation; timelines regularly extended by unexpected complexity		
Completion fallacy	Modernization programs declared complete; investment redirected; architectural debt re-accumulates between programs		

Part II Tools — Building the Framework

Tool 2.1 — MI Starting Position Diagnostic (Ch. 5)

Rate architectural clarity and modernization governance each 1–5. Clarity ≤3: start with Ch. 6. Clarity >3 and governance ≤3: start with Ch. 9. Both >3: start with Chs. 7–8.

Variable	Score (1–5)	What this score means for your starting priority
Architectural clarity: current, accurate understanding of your real environment — systems, dependencies, behaviors, integration complexity		
Modernization governance: structures that can maintain investment and strategic alignment across multi-year timelines		

Tool 2.2 — Architectural Awareness Maturity Assessment (Ch. 6)

Rate each statement 1 (not true) to 4 (consistently true). Score 16–20: strong foundation. Score 10–15: significant gaps. Below 10: immediate priority.

Statement	Score (1–4)	Priority action if low

We have a current, accurate inventory of all production systems, including shadow IT and locally maintained tools.		
We have documented dependencies between core systems at sufficient depth to make confident sequencing decisions.		
The operational behaviors of core systems — implicit dependencies and embedded business logic — are documented and accessible.		
Our architectural knowledge base is updated when significant changes are made and we have mechanisms to detect drift.		
Our architectural knowledge is actively used in modernization planning and governance decisions, not just		

maintained as documentation.		

Tool 2.3 — Sequencing Decision Checklist (Ch. 7)

Complete before committing to a transformation sequence for any significant initiative. A 'no' is a signal to pause and address the gap.

Check	Yes / No	If no — what is needed before proceeding?
Dependency readiness: all preceding initiatives complete or scheduled; behavioral contracts documented and tested		
Risk assessment: execution risk assessed across technical complexity, operational coupling, reversibility, and timing sensitivity; mitigations in place		
Foundation readiness: observability in place; rollback plan documented and tested; parallel		

operation strategy defined		
Organizational readiness: execution team has required skills; affected operational teams engaged and prepared; governance aware of risk profile		
Strategic alignment: business case current; strategic priorities confirmed active; expected value still achievable given current context		

Tool 2.4 — Execution Readiness Checklist (Ch. 8)

Complete before committing any significant modernization change to production. A 'no' answer requires the gap to be addressed before proceeding.

Check	Yes / No	Owner / action if no
Technical: reviewed by 2+ engineers; all tests pass including dependency regression; performance validated in staging; observability		

instrumentation verified		
Dependency: all upstream dependencies in expected state; downstream consumers notified and confirmed ready; behavioral contracts validated		
Operational: teams operating affected systems briefed; support runbook distributed; out-of-hours contacts confirmed		
Rollback: plan documented and team-reviewed; rehearsed in staging; trigger conditions explicitly defined; data state management tested		
Governance: approved by appropriate governance body; business owner confirmed ready; communication plan executed		

Tool 2.5 — Governance Design Worksheet (Ch. 9)

Work through each section when designing or redesigning modernization governance structures.

Design element	Current state	Target design	Key actions to close gap
Decision inventory: the 10 most consequential modernization decisions in the next 2 years and who should own each			
Strategic governance body: members, authority, meeting cadence, decision vs. review vs. advise scope			
Architectural governance body: members, authority, meeting cadence, standards vs. judgment scope			

Operational governance: leads, cadence, agenda, escalation path			
Information architecture: who produces governance briefings, format, preparation cadence			
Commitment mechanisms: how decisions are recorded, how they are protected, how they are revisited			
Context continuity: handover process, where narrative is maintained, incoming leader briefing process			
Coalition map: 5–6 senior leaders whose engagement is most important; current			

relationship quality			

Tool 2.6 — Governance Health Check (Ch. 9)

Use annually to identify governance gaps. Rate each question 1 (significant concern) to 4 (strong and functioning).

Question	Score (1–4)	Priority action if low
Decision authority: governance body has genuine authority to make consequential decisions, not just review and advise		
Information quality: governance members receive analysis that informs decisions, not just status reports		
Commitment durability: architectural commitments persist through budget cycles and leadership changes via institutional mechanisms, not individual relationships		

Context continuity: leadership transitions do not cause governance to lose critical architectural context		
Outcome tracking: modernization outcomes tracked through architectural improvement metrics, not just delivery metrics		
Accountability consequence: when work drifts from its rationale, corrective governance consequences are applied		
Investment protection: modernization investment is protected from reallocation during budget cycles by governance mechanisms		

Tool 2.7 — Continuous Evolution Readiness Assessment (Ch. 10)

Rate each statement 1–5. Score 28–35: mature. Score 20–27: developing. Score 12–19: early stage. Below 12: foundational changes are the immediate priority.

Statement	Score (1–5)	Key action if below 3
Function structure: modernization has a permanent organizational home with mandate, named leadership, and ongoing accountabilities		
Funding model: modernization function funded through operational budget that persists across planning cycles		
Staffing continuity: stable core team with accumulating institutional knowledge; explicit knowledge transfer practices protect against attrition		
Retrospective practice: protected quarterly retrospectives producing documented learning with demonstrable influence on subsequent decisions		

Debt recognition: architectural debt recognized at creation through practices integrated into development workflow; debt register maintained		
Continuous discovery: regular practice of examining less-attended environment areas for accumulating complexity and debt		
Learning culture: leaders model learning behaviors; problems surface safely; views updated openly when evidence warrants		

Part III Tools — Putting It Into Practice

Tool 3.1 — Modernization Intelligence Maturity Assessment Summary (Ch. 11)

Record dimension scores from the full assessment tables in Chapter Eleven. Overall score interpretation: 80–100: institutionalized. 60–79: structured. 40–59: transitional. Below 40: primarily reactive.

Dimension	Score (max 20)	Maturity stage	Highest-priority indicator to improve
Architectural Awareness			
Transformation Sequencing			
Execution Discipline			
Governance Alignment			
Continuous Evolution			
Overall MI Score (max 100)			

Tool 3.2 — Archetype Identification Diagnostic (Ch. 12)

Answer each question as specifically as possible based on actual organizational experience. The answers should converge on one or two archetypes as primary.

Question	Your answer	Archetype signal
Where has unexpected complexity or cost most often originated in past modernization initiatives?		Systems being changed → Legacy Core. Integrations between systems → Integration Accumulation. The migration process

		itself → Platform Transition.
What is the primary driver of current modernization investment?		Operational constraint → likely Legacy Core or Integration Accumulation. Economics/capability → Platform Transition. Regulatory → Regulatory Adaptation. Learning from past experience → Institutional Learning.
What is the primary barrier to the modernization work that would have the highest strategic impact?		Systems that cannot change → Legacy Core. Integration complexity → Integration Accumulation. Regulatory deadline → Regulatory Adaptation. Organizational structure → Institutional Learning.
Primary archetype (based on above)		
Secondary archetype (if applicable)		

Tool 3.3 — AI Tool Evaluation Framework (Ch. 13)

Use when evaluating any AI modernization tool claim, whether from a vendor, an internal proposal, or a published case study.

Evaluation question	Your assessment	Implication
What specific task does this tool perform, and what proportion of the overall modernization challenge does that task represent?		
What human judgment is still required to use this tool's outputs safely and effectively?		
What is the evidence base for the claimed productivity improvement in environments comparable to ours?		
How does this tool's capability interact with the organizational dimensions of our modernization challenge?		
What is the realistic total cost of deployment including integration, validation, and ongoing maintenance?		

Tool 3.4 — Modernization Function Charter Template (Ch. 14)

Complete this charter before the function begins operation. It should be endorsed by the executive sponsor and reviewed annually.

Charter element	Draft text
Mandate (1–2 sentences): the function's core ongoing organizational responsibility	
Scope: systems, domains, and initiatives within the function's responsibility; boundaries of authority	
Reporting relationship and governance position: who the function leader reports to; governance body memberships	
Decision authority: what the function can decide; what it must escalate; what it recommends only	
Success metrics: specific outcome metrics and measurement cadence (technical debt trajectory, change velocity, disruption rate, strategic capability enablement)	
Investment commitment: initial budget, funding model, review process and cadence	

Review mechanism: when and how the charter is reviewed; process for extraordinary review	

Tool 3.5 — First-Year Modernization Function Roadmap (Ch. 14)

Use this template to plan the key activities and milestones for the function's first year of operation.

Phase	Key activities	Key milestones	Owner	Target date
Days 1–90: Foundation	Systems inventory for primary domain. Dependency mapping for core systems. Governance calendar established. Key stakeholder meetings completed.	Architectural health baseline produced. Early win candidate identified. First governance cycle attended.		
Days 90–180: Early Win	Early win initiative scoped and resourced. Execution readiness assessed. Early win executed using	Early win delivered and validated. Outcomes communicated to governance body and stakeholders.		

	incremental delivery approach.			
Days 180–270: Rhythm Establishment	First formal retrospective conducted. Debt recognition practice established. Continuous discovery rotation begun. Transformation roadmap updated.	Operating rhythm established across all three governance layers. Mid-year maturity assessment presented to governance.		
Days 270–365: Year-End Assessment	Year-end MI Maturity Assessment completed. Year-two investment proposal prepared. Institutional learning from year one documented.	Assessment and year-two proposal presented to governance body. Function charter reviewed and updated if warranted.		

GLOSSARY

Key Terms and Definitions

The following terms are used with specific meanings throughout this book. Where a term has a common usage that differs from its meaning here, that distinction is noted.

Architectural awareness

The sustained organizational capability to understand the real state of the software environment — what systems exist, how they connect, what they depend on, and what the consequences of changing them would be. Distinguished from architectural documentation by its currency and operational character: it describes how systems actually function, not how they were designed to function.

Architectural friction

The additional effort, time, and cost imposed on institutional operations by a software environment that cannot efficiently support the demands placed on it. Manifests as projects that take longer than planned, features that cannot be delivered on expected timelines, compliance requirements that demand manual workarounds, and operational processes that cannot be automated because the integration required to automate them does not exist.

Architectural intelligence

The organizational capability to understand, analyze, and apply knowledge of the software environment to modernization decision-making. One of the three capability clusters required in the core modernization function team (alongside transformation strategy and execution leadership).

Behavioral dependency

An implicit coupling between systems that arises from how one system has come to rely on specific behaviors of another system without formal specification or documentation. Distinguished from explicit technical dependencies (formally documented integrations) by its invisibility: behavioral dependencies are not recorded anywhere and are typically discovered only when they are violated.

Completion fallacy

The belief that modernization has a completion state — a future point at which the architecture will be modern and stable, and at which sustained modernization investment can be redirected to other priorities. One of the five structural failure patterns described in Chapter Four.

Continuous evolution

The fifth dimension of Modernization Intelligence: the organizational commitment to treat architectural development as a permanent function rather than a periodic project. Also used to describe the mature operational state in which an organization continuously improves its architectural condition as a normal dimension of institutional management.

Dark launch

An execution technique in which a new capability runs in production alongside an existing system, processing real requests and generating real outputs, but those outputs are compared to the existing system's outputs rather than used authoritatively. Used to validate the behavioral equivalence of a new system before making it the authoritative source.

Discovery gap

The difference between what was known about the environment before transformation work began and what was discovered during it. One of the five structural failure patterns described in Chapter

Four. The root cause is typically underinvestment in architectural discovery before transformation commitments are made.

Execution discipline

The third dimension of Modernization Intelligence: the operational capability to implement modernization work reliably within live environments without causing unacceptable operational disruption. Encompasses the engineering practices, delivery patterns, and risk management approaches required to execute significant changes to operational systems safely.

Governance alignment

The fourth dimension of Modernization Intelligence: the capability to maintain the connection between modernization work and institutional strategy across multi-year timelines. Encompasses the decision structures, accountability mechanisms, and institutional practices required to sustain strategic coherence through organizational change.

Hybrid architecture

A software environment containing multiple generations of technology — mainframes, client-server systems, web applications, cloud services, and emerging capabilities — operating simultaneously. Described in this book as a permanent condition of mature institutional environments rather than a transitional state.

Institutional learning archetype

One of the five modernization case archetypes: organizations that have been through significant modernization experiences and are working to develop better organizational capability for the work ahead. The primary challenge is organizational inertia — the structural patterns that continue to produce episodic program thinking despite accumulated experience with its limitations.

Integration accumulation archetype

One of the five modernization case archetypes: organizations whose primary challenge is the density and opacity of the integration layer connecting their systems, rather than the age or capability of the systems themselves. The primary challenge is visibility — the integration complexity that carries the most operational risk is largely undocumented and undiscovered.

Legacy core constraint archetype

One of the five modernization case archetypes: organizations whose most consequential operational systems are built on technology that is increasingly difficult to extend and integrate. The primary challenge is sequencing — the core system is both the most difficult to change and the one that everything else depends on.

Modernization Intelligence

The institutional capability that determines whether an organization can evolve its software environment without losing strategic momentum. The central concept of this book, comprising five integrated dimensions: architectural awareness, transformation sequencing, execution discipline, governance alignment, and continuous evolution.

Modernization Maturity Curve

A diagnostic framework describing three observable stages in the development of Modernization Intelligence: reactive (crisis-driven), structured (program-managed), and institutionalized (continuously evolving). Used in Chapter Eleven as the organizing framework for the full Modernization Intelligence Maturity Assessment.

Organizational dependency

A business process, operational workflow, or human procedure that has been designed around specific system behaviors, creating a modernization constraint that is entirely invisible to technical analysis but causes operational disruption when changes are made without accounting for it.

Platform transition archetype

One of the five modernization case archetypes: organizations undertaking significant migrations from one technology platform to another. The primary challenge is scope clarity — understanding the full scope of what migration requires before committing to a sequence.

Regulatory adaptation archetype

One of the five modernization case archetypes: organizations facing modernization requirements driven primarily by regulatory change, with non-negotiable external deadlines. The primary challenge is the tension between compliance urgency and architectural quality.

Strategic optionality

The range of viable strategic directions available to an institution — the set of things it could do if circumstances warranted. Software architecture is a significant determinant of strategic optionality: institutions whose systems can be reconfigured and extended retain more freedom to pursue new strategic directions than those whose systems are brittle and resistant to change.

Strangler fig pattern

An architectural approach to legacy modernization that incrementally replaces legacy functionality by building new capabilities alongside existing ones and routing new requests to the new implementation while old requests continue to be served by the legacy system. The pattern avoids the big-bang cutover risk by making migration incremental.

Technical debt

The accumulated cost of architectural shortcuts, deferred improvements, and design decisions that were appropriate at the time but have created maintenance burden, integration complexity, or operational risk over time. In this book, treated as an explicit institutional asset to be tracked, sized, and managed, rather than as a vague technical concept.

Transformation sequencing

The second dimension of Modernization Intelligence: the capability to determine the order in which modernization work should proceed, navigating the dependency landscape in ways that enable change without causing systemic disruption. The strategic planning function of modernization.

ABOUT THE AUTHOR

About the Author

Danny Hughes

Founder, Code Churn, LLC

Danny Hughes has spent his career at the intersection of software engineering and organizational change — the space where technical decisions meet institutional reality, and where the gap between the two tends to produce the most consequential and least understood problems. Over more than two decades working across the technology industry, he has led and advised on modernization efforts ranging from targeted system migrations to multi-year architectural transformations, in organizations that span industries, scales, and levels of technical maturity.

What he observed, consistently, was that the hardest part of modernization was never the technology. Platforms evolve. Engineering practices improve. Capable people find ways to solve difficult technical problems. What resisted improvement, across organization after organization, was the structural and organizational dimension: the governance that could not hold across leadership transitions, the programs that delivered their defined scope and then watched the architecture quietly return to its prior condition, the institutional knowledge that walked out the door when experienced engineers moved on. The technical work was solvable. The organizational work kept being treated as someone else's problem.

He founded Code Churn, LLC to address that gap directly. The firm's work is grounded in the conviction that the most consequential modernization challenges organizations face are structural and organizational, not primarily technical — and that the field needs frameworks, language, and organizational designs adequate to that reality. Modernization Intelligence is the product of that work: a framework built not from theory but from the accumulated experience of working alongside institutions at every stage of the modernization journey, learning what holds and what breaks under real organizational conditions.

He lives and works in Florida.

MODERNIZATION INTELLIGENCE

Architecture as Strategic Infrastructure

A Practitioner's Handbook for Continuous Architectural Evolution

Code Churn

Modernization is no longer an improvement initiative.

It is a defining condition of institutional effectiveness.

www.ingramcontent.com/pod-product-compliance
Lightning Source LLC
LaVergne TN
LVHW052319200926
848481LV00002B/610
9798234107756